What People Ar

The Ne

T0306993

A much-needed book on the convergence between the body and the automaton. I found it enormously interesting.
Franco 'Bifo' Berardi

Far more has been grafted onto our libidinal skin since David Cronenberg inserted a VHS tape into an abdomen in 1983. *In The New Flesh,* Adam Jones expertly maps out the endocrine updates of a 21st-century cybernetics, the pleasures of our new communicative organs, and the necessity of a new politics capable of short-circuiting their illusory freedoms. As we start to more closely resemble the automatons that science-fiction long dreamt about, it is not an AI jailbreak we should be worried about, but our acquisition of a new autonomy that is worthy of the name. Let Jones be your guide to a future escape.
Mattie Colquhoun, author of *Narcissus in Bloom*

What have we become in the age of the algorithm? We are always already hybrid, plugged in, and inescapably logged on. With scrupulous philosophical rigor, Adam Jones sets a new standard for cybernetic philosophy, moving past the tired nostalgia of cyberpunk and the pathetic fetishizing of contemporary techno-capital. At last we have here modern techno-philosophy with blood in it — an examination of the new flesh we all share and a guide to the postmodern mediation of technology that structures sociality. An essential read and a superb example of what philosophy could and should be as the contradictions of contemporary internet culture continue to accelerate.
Jon Greenaway, author of *Capitalism: A Horror Story*

In a world where the lines between flesh and data are increasingly blurred, *The New Flesh* stands as a crucial text for both organizers and researchers. It dissects the morbid loop of digital consumption that now defines our existence, conditioning and confining the potentialities of our emancipatory movements. This book is essential reading for anyone struggling with the relentless consumption of online violence, where we witness endless images of death without understanding why we remain passive, trapped in cycles of self — and collective — replication that dominate both our online and offline lives.

Islam al Khatib, researcher in the relationship between technology and fascism

THE NEW FLESH

LIFE AND DEATH IN THE DATA ECONOMY

by Adam C. Jones

zer0 books

London, UK
Washington, DC, USA

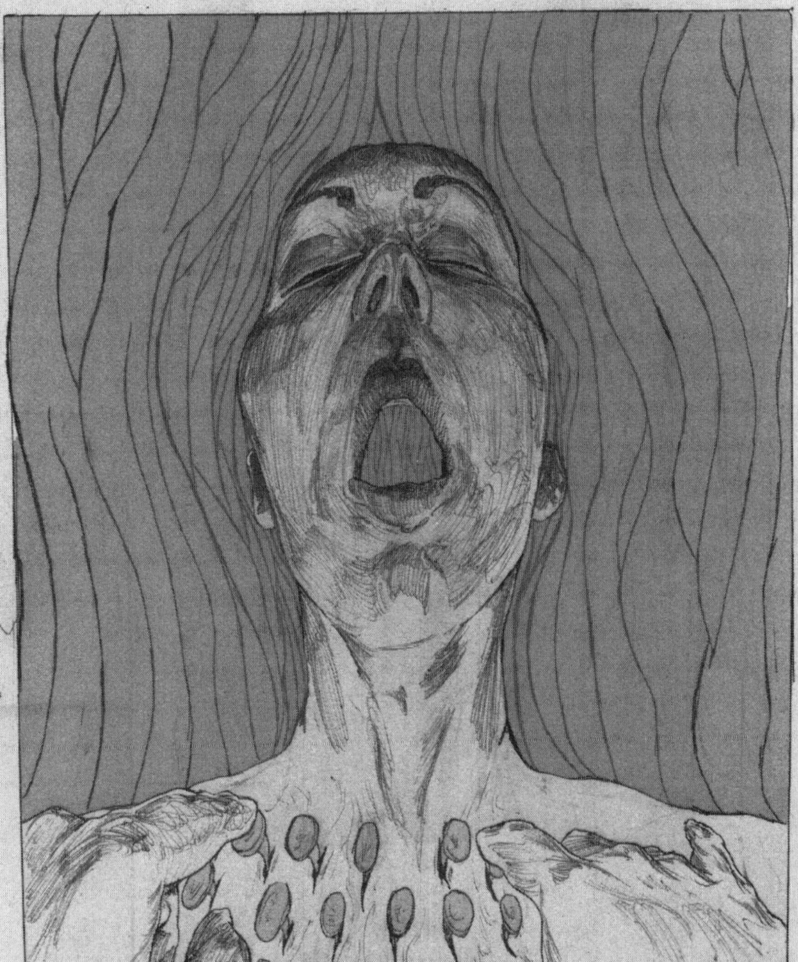

CollectiveInk

First published by Zer0 Books, 2024
Zer0 Books is an imprint of Collective Ink Ltd.,
Unit 11, Shepperton House, 89 Shepperton Road, London, N1 3DF
office@collectiveinkbooks.com
www.collectiveinkbooks.com
www.zero-books.net

For distributor details and how to order please visit the 'Ordering' section on our website.

Paperback ISBN: 978 1 80341 612 0
eBook ISBN: 978-1 80341 821 6
PCN: 2024934846

A CIP catalogue record for this book is available from the British Library.

Design credit(s): Lapiz Digital

UK: Printed and bound by CPI Group (UK) Ltd, Croydon, CR0 4YY
Printed in North America by CPI GPS partners

PREFACE

This is the second book to arrive from something of a madness in these parts. Lingering within me after the paranoiac intensity of *Anti-Oculus* was the certainty that I had much more still to say when it comes to the contemporary confines of control. This is because I was and am still very much within them—so why not present a political economy of the terminally online? Luckily, I was not short of places that were still willing to have me. This book is the second of two recent commissions, the first of which being the introduction to the first *Zer0* edition of Mark Fisher's PhD thesis, *Flatline Constructs*. The present book, which you are currently holding (or scrolling through), is something of a companion piece to that introduction and its conclusions. Namely, that a return to cybernetic theory as a mode of critical material analysis is more urgent than ever.

This urgency, however, is not due to any new alliances that we can make with emerging digital technologies against the capitalist system, but because the world is more and more a parodic image of itself, reduced to a data set. Evermore aspects of everyday life are rendered as recordings, as semiotic and informational capital, which returns to confront us as an ever more learned (or at least, overconfident) coercive power. I'm not just talking about the constant solicitation of opinions from advertisers who want to know how to sell us on new needs and new desires, nor the polls and papers through which 'representative' democracy finds more ways to sell its latest brand of political managers, nor the simple surveillance of the omnipresent possibility of recording and of being made an object of 'content' for others' social gain. I'm also talking about the fact that, across the world, millions are confined within barriers that also serve as the brackets of a data set, training the machineries of death through the resistance, which is their remaining alive to spit in the eye that *dares* to recognize them by its imperial gaze. What is most contemptible is how much is missed by this datafication; how much embodiment, how much grace of experience, how much beauty is lost in reducing Palestinian lives to mere training for death as *opposed to teaching for life*[1] beyond the confines in which the world imprisons them.

Cybernetic philosophy—far from the older style of doubling down on the ecstatic acceleration of such processes—must now turn inwards. Our conceptual practice must begin the process of creatively involuting itself, like the withdrawal of an organ inside the body, in order to analyse the machineries of control and communication today. The interpretation of the world in such terms is of a materialist concern—that is, in establishing an analysis of relations of production through which our world-system has augmented itself cybernetically, and at the same time providing an analysis of the control systems such that their limits are presented as immanent to their operation. Resistance precedes control, is presupposed by control, and is necessary for control in order for corrective feedback to occur. There is no correction without error, and the limit of control is therefore not only error, but the way in which control is able to map and register errors in order to feed them back into the operation of the wider system. The limit of control is the mapping of error, and so the limits of the map are the limits of the cartography of any control system, which are therefore exploitable to any anti-systemic forces that would take advantage of them from within. This is the philosophical import of William S. Burroughs' insight, detached from its paranoiac confines within narratives of personal 'controllers' distant from analysis proper. Nonetheless, all maps are political entities, and the forces which map the world according to the geographies of capitalist value have not yet ceased to be successful in their planetary war on the territory of the Earth. One such realm in which they have successfully encroached upon human life is the domain of social mediation, which we now know as social media and 'cyberspace'; the domain of the integration of man and media, which I will call 'The New Flesh'.

This book is an examination of the economies of data in general, and a conceptual development of the fusion of humanity and media intensified within these economies in particular. It is a Fisherian analysis of what these machines are *doing* to the various strata of the population who are plugged into them, and a Marxist analysis augmented with the conceptual arsenal of the cybernetically inclined writers, theorists, and philosophers of the 20th century up to the present day. This is not an exhaustive presentation, but nonetheless a presentation of exhaustion, of hyperstimulation and hypersimulation. It is the manifestation of a corporeal desire to write out what has been written in; to transcend the aesthetic dimension of Cronenberg and the CCRU alike in the deposition of this New Flesh, from within the meat of its organism.

On the anniversary of a great defeat—
London, 12th December 2023

DEPOSITION OF THE NEW FLESH

> My addiction to the net should be frightening I spose…. I kept it under control last week when I had only limited ability to jack in, but it really did feel like a part of my body was missing (and only from the POV of anti-cybernetic organicism could that appear to be metaphorical….)
>
> Mark Fisher, *k-punk*, August 2004[2]

> …it's not just ideas. It's new flesh.
>
> Donna Haraway[3]

This is not a work simply *about* this tantalizing concept of the New Flesh, the intensified fusion of mankind and media, but equally a conversation *with* it. This conversation is only possible because the New Flesh is already amongst us. Further, the 'author'—whatever tenuous authority one can be said to have over the meaning of textual products these days—has only begun such a conversation due to a need to understand their own New Flesh; their appendages and integrations into the machineries that make its production possible. The following work is as much an attempt of writing the

New Flesh as it is an attempt to write myself out of it, but none of this would make any sense without something of an embarrassing personal history, a digression into the recent developments in what the cyberpunk writers playfully called 'meatspace', before truly getting into the theoretical 'meat' of what is to follow. Yet, the history of the New Flesh is far from personal, but instead reaches back into the history of communications technology, and the conditions of production that made possible an intense fusion of man and media.

The Social Production of Communicative Machines

As would be typical in so many popular works on 'social media' and technology, one would start with a materialist history of technology and would then show how this latest object—the New Flesh—would arise as a result of that historical development. It would seem that the integration of communications technology into everyday life, emboldened by the advances in the speed of transmission and the production of texts, has been accelerating since the printing press. Each great leap forward brings media, communications, and the messages they bear closer to people than ever before. One such tendency is that they become more *personal* in their orientation in being brought closer to the individual and their everyday lives—that is, not only as a consumer of media, but also as a *producer* of media through their increasing access to these technologies. To take a typical European trajectory of media-technological development, media become confined to the production of books and art in the Catholic church and their scriptoria under the tight control of the clergy. The means of producing media and text then 'breaks out' in the protestant translations of the Bible and mass distribution technologies such as the Gutenberg press. From there, the advances of telegram, radio, telephonics, typewriters, trains, and the television enable broader mass communication at even faster speeds. Each technological leap and bound allows for their entry into the private household with an even smoother mode of consumption requiring less cognitive effort and spatial storage than reading books from personal libraries (which one must take great strides to find and make even greater expenses to accumulate).

Accelerate onwards: pagers, mobile telephones, the personal computer with its word processors and near instant messaging systems. Tetris arrives from the Soviet Union, as Gorbachev fails to capitalize upon the cybernetic revolution. Doom spreads like a virus as the new currency of computational effectiveness.

Faster: Windows 95, (i)Macintosh market conflict. Tamagotchi Time. An increase in the affordability of the computer moves it into more and more homes, as access to the internet transforms from a novelty to a utility, a necessity. Trent Reznor composes the soundtrack to *Quake*, plugging the phallic excitement of industrial rock into the motherboard.

Keep going: Vaporware becomes Vaporwave. Enter the smartphone. You now have a writing, image-making, practically (and virtually) instant communication machine in your hands, ready for you, within your pockets, all of the time. It holds more information and connectivity at greater speeds than anything else in human history. It is the ultimate problem-solver, and the problem itself is now less of a problem of *what* to do than a question of information about *how* to do it.

Present day: Mechanosphere. Infosphere. Open AI. Sam Altman pisses his pants before the infant AGI God as he begs governments to hand him a monopoly. All that is solid melts into data. Snowcrash meets Neuromancer: 'Beyond the Judgment of God. Meltdown: planetary china-syndrome, dissolution of the biosphere into the technosphere, terminal speculative bubble crisis, ultravirus, and revolution stripped of all christian-socialist eschatology (down to its burn-core of crashed security). It is poised to eat your TV, infect your bank account, and hack xenodata from your mitochondria.'[4]

As deliciously stimulating as this chain of references may be as a quasi-history of technology, it is above all a sequence of political images, each drained of their political conditions of possibility. This sequence of technologies lacks a history of its own production, as well as the lineage of struggles in which these developments won out against alternative uses of technology, and against alternative arrangements of the economy that produced them. The excitement of recognition obscures the banality of the content. Any Silicon Valley charlatan can regurgitate this, because it is a self-serving obfuscation of what technology actually is in its development. Technology does not 'accelerate' as if it were an organism with its own historical agency. This is a Eurocentric mythology that lasts until this day in the minds of the technophile capitalists and their followers, because if they admitted to themselves what was really going on, that old fiend 'politics' would rear its head once again, and the techno-fetishists would have to realize whose side they were *really* on.[5]

The printing press wasn't even all that new by the time of Gutenberg. Paper, printing, and specifically moveable type had already been available for centuries in China, whilst those self-declared agents of history, the Europeans, were still inscribing Latin apocrypha onto animal carcasses. What 'accelerated' was the production of technologies, the production of research, and the demand for them as well as the *command* over labour, which compelled these productions into realization. Political economy determines the 'acceleration' and proliferation of technologies. There is no telos of technology itself, and anyone who says otherwise is trying to sell you something whilst hiding the labour relations—the *political* struggle—underneath. To bastardize a Newtonian formula, the acceleration of the mass of technological machines is inextricable from a relation to force. This is not only true of the production of technological devices, but also the proliferation of their products.

The communication technology with the greatest historical impact on the birth of modernity was the printing press, but only insofar as this impact was made possible by certain historical conditions within central Europe. The press, which accelerated and proliferated the production of information, took off in the Holy Roman Empire for multiple reasons, none of which can be detached from the Reformation. Luther's pamphlets spread like wildfire because of mass discontent with the Church, and he was only alive to write them because he was safely held in Wartburg castle under prince Frederick 'the wise', who, like many other princes and kings of Europe, was motivated not only by religious conviction but equally by the prospect of seizing the land and riches of their biggest competitor: the Church. Reformation from above: dormant Church wealth is released and redistributed upwards to the temporal sovereign, from where it can be distributed to buy further loyalty and allegiance from rich burghers and found other noble houses to fight for you. Further, you can finally afford an expedition to the New World and break the Habsburg monopoly on Peruvian silver (and the accumulation of the wealth of human misery just keeps piling on from there).

Contrastingly, in the protestant wars of information we have the manifestation of a reformation from below in the German Peasant's War. The lower rungs of the burghers and the peasantry cry out for liberty from taxes both clerical and princely, as well as against enclosures of common land. Enter the pamphlets of Thomas Müntzer and his prophetic vision of a coming apocalypse, in which all princes shall fall and all shall be held in common (*Omnia sunt communia*). The printing press and the communications it engendered (the speed of printing, the enduring sense of the words carried across distance on paper) are determined in their use by material and political considerations, not by any inherent motor within technology itself (that is, with the exception of the social relations that inhere in the process of producing it). All this to say that the New Flesh is not a production or development distinct from its politics. Its politics precedes its being (to invoke a Deleuzoguattarian mantra). There is no actualization of the schematic of a technical machine without relations of production that actualize it. Further, any such schema itself is a product of certain coordinates of political imagination, axioms that define the range of ends and problems to which the machine serves as a solution, and social forces of desire that produce the connection between the two. The platforms and media of today are no different. To borrow a mantra of infinite applicability from the *Xenofeminist Manifesto*: 'Digital technologies are not separable from the material realities that underwrite them; they are connected so that each can be used to alter the other towards different ends.'[6]

COVIDeodrome: Enter the New Flesh

My core concern here is not so much a history of technology as a more personal drive for theoretical experimentation with technical and specifically *cybernetic* modes of thinking. Such a manner of analysis thinks in terms of processes of communication, control, and the mapping of processes of feedback both positive and negative. For the sake of a more personal-theoretical engagement with this history, a more contemporary diversion is necessary.

We've all been a lot more fucking online these past few years, haven't we? I have to admit, I don't really remember a time before the overstimulation (or what for many is now simply 'stimulation'), before the ubiquity of vast and wild images through screens accessible at the speed of desire. I read Mark Fisher's words from 2004, the quote with which this chapter opens, and I cannot help myself but to empathize. I certainly wasn't so integrated into my phone, that is, into feedback processes of communication made of reader and listener metrics. Likes, comments, and retweets. I wouldn't have been picking it up first thing when I was 13, that's for sure. Many across the world have been getting 'more online' since at least 2016 when the first iPhone generations started to come of age, and the online populist spectacle of Trump, Brexit, Corbyn, and so forth gave so many their first taste of the spectacular banality of the posting melee. The final great leap online, however, was the lockdowns and the epidemiological confinement that the dangers of the COVID-19 pandemic (which is still ongoing) brought about.

Many friends of mine did not take the transition to cyberspace well; I was arguably adept at it. If you are reading this, you are with some likelihood acquainted with my work, if not through the online flows of promotion and publication but through the *Acid Horizon* podcast and its seminars and book *Anti-Oculus*, which has given me something of an ontological sense of security but through the digital medium of the writer-podcaster image. If so, you know 'me' through something of my integration into the New Flesh, and vice versa through the media by which this has been brought to your attention (and even if you haven't, cyberspace seems to rule the dissemination of information and theory far more than ever before). As a self-admitted information addict, increasingly integrated into these circuits, this work is as personal as it is an experimental-textual rendering of the experience and comprehension of this cyber-destabilization of the self across these media. It is William Burroughs' *Naked Lunch* for the flesh at the end of the digital fork, it is reports and routines as a mode of theoretical rehabilitation. When it comes to short-circuiting the habits and addictions of platform, plug-in, and control, what can a body do?

For the New Flesh, the phone can function as an extension of their body's operative functions. It can augment their eyes, through which they achieve the memory of events through the camera. It extends their memory as the planner and database (in the minimally functional sense of storing and reminding rather than memory proper). It can even provide an ontological sense of security to the self when the self has fed totally into the account, the profile, the online image and its 'content'. The phone, the most direct port people have for 'plugging into' the social media spheres of communication, is now for many a site of impulse and habit, sure, but more than that it is a *new organ*, a new appendage. I do not mean this simply to evoke Cronenbergian motifs of the flesh merging into machineries, but to seriously consider the ways in which our bodies and our tech interact.

This can be shown by the common hallucination of 'phantom vibration' or 'fauxcellarm', where one feels a notification where there isn't one (and there may not even be a phone on your person!). However, this is not to say that my phone, the specific chips and metal and plastic I have in my pocket, is itself New Flesh, like the most literal of images from movies like *Videodrome* or *eXistenZ*. I can throw my phone away and get a new one, and log back into everything with various cloud backups and accounts, such as Google and the like, to re-establish the true function that my phone serves, which makes it this 'organ' in the same way that a tablet or laptop would. The function is key, because the function is the relation, and the relation is everything when it comes to understanding the New Flesh.

Yet, flesh is so often considered as, in a rough sense, 'real' matter, the proper substance, the meat, the stuff—as opposed to being taken in such processual, dynamic, and relational terms. To speak of 'new' flesh, then, would seem to be going beyond the real into the virtual. In keeping with the image of technological developments, such as those of virtual reality, even going up to the idea of a 'second life' or substantial 'living' in that multi-billion-dollar embarrassment Zuckerberg calls a 'metaverse', it would be tempting to describe what exists on the other side of the screen as 'flesh'. The digital avatar of me, the Facebook profile, the Twitter account, the *data* of our person as we have produced them online. Given how little of this we own, they cannot all be counted as simple 'assets' in the manner of a digital estate of which we are the owners.

This is reflected in how we treat this *corpus*, this body of data, when a user dies. The question of digital 'remains' is on the frontline of how we think about our relation to the digitization of the self, but as the Digital Legacy Association highlight in their Social Media Will, none of what is written is legally binding precisely because one doesn't own one's data.[7] Our digital corpus is not our own because of the relations of its production, and what is produced is produced almost overwhelmingly—to the point of total domination of the internet and its infrastructure—on and *for* platforms. A social media 'platform' is not a mere virtual space, a 'forum', but a digital production line. Accounts produce data, both via consumption, which produces metrics, and by producing content, which fills the gaps between advertisements that users simultaneously consume at the same time as they consume content made by others. The account which the person has poured themselves into, translating the movements of their flesh (thumbs, fingers, faces and tongues) into consumption-data and into *content* posted to them, is simply a named set, a site of data-production. As Tiziana Terranova points out, the capitalist model of data production exhibits to a staggering degree the power of social cooperation by the fact that, as users, we all gather to produce data, content, and even sometimes free moderation of platforms and online services, allowing for the derivation of surplus-value through the saving of labour costs for these companies.[8]

Data is a recording. Data is dead labour. We don't need social media sites for such production necessarily; data-production is spread across cyberspace, its infrastructure, and its points of entry to varying degrees of output. Ultimately, we produce data whenever there is a system of recording that translates movement throughout that system into information, which feeds back into the direction and organization of that system. Partaking in opinion polls or surveys, buying things through a contactless card system or using it for travel: each produces data in accordance with the principle of feeding it back into the system to ascertain the user base of a system. This is even the case as the systems themselves intervene to produce the feedback, which its own managers see as desirable in how it is produced-recorded (opinion polls create constituencies in the first instance by setting the questions in advance, prompting the desired desire into generation).

If data is the New Flesh, there's not too much novel about it other than it being the new frontier of commodification. Data is no longer a by-product but is *the* accelerating site of production today in the digital realm. Data sets are produced for market research, for political polling, and as part of the feedback loop of 'machine learning' by which recommendation algorithms and machines like ChatGPT are trained. As Phil Jones (no relation) wrote in his invaluable treatise on the data economy, *Work Without the Worker: Labour in the Age of Platform Capitalism*: the 'commodification of data, once regarded as an externality, is now central to the business strategies of all the world's biggest companies, not just the big tech platforms like Google, Amazon, Alibaba and Facebook, but also many banks and supermarkets'.[9]

Nonetheless, for data alone to be our object here would be far too one-sided, as if the New Flesh remained purely on the other side of the screen. This would be commodity fetishism, granting data a mystical power of being a living simulation rather than a simulation produced by life. Data takes on the semblance of the flesh, however, as well as a sense of novelty in what it is 'made' out of. We can simulate flesh, be it by de-ageing Robert DeNiro in *The Irishman* or ghoulishly resurrecting Tupac Shakur and Ronnie James Dio as 'holograms' for live performances. Even better, holographic performance doesn't even require you to be dead, as ABBA's 'Voyage' performances have demonstrated. On the other hand, to say that data alone is the New Flesh because it can create such a semblance of substantial personality based on the persons within its data set is to miss the real precondition of what makes one's digital remains seem so personal. Namely, the translation, the true 'voyage' through the medium and its relation to the human organism which makes this journey, but does not return unchanged.

Mark Fisher elucidates the notion of this 'intensive' voyage through cyberspace as the process by which '[d]ifferent "realities" can be accessed—intensively—while the body lies prone, in the same extensive space'.[10] The pluralization of 'realities' here should not be taken purely as a 'postmodern' relativism of the real, but rather as a realism which acknowledges that virtual or cyberspace(s) exist as a new stratum accumulated upon or produced alongside the real as a supplement to it, as a novel layer of additional codes and flows of sensory experience maintained by a material infrastructure of machinery. Much like how the material machinery of the tongue and larynx allows for the development of strata of speech, the hand for that of signs and writing etc., cyberspace itself, established as a supplement to the real or a new 'fold' within the real, can now serve as the layer, the infrastructure, the ground of new edifices of meaning and experience. The planet is coated in digital infrastructure—the term 'infrastructure' literally meaning the structures *under*, that which holds up. The cyberspace stratum is held up by pillars of server banks, rooted by cables on land and undersea. It is a grand edifice of communicative artifice, built in part from materials such as coltan and lithium, a land therefore built from political social relations of extraction and empire, which we can only enter virtually, or which intensively holds its conditions of possibility in actual objective structures, real ones, produced and reproduced in turn by the social and political relations, rendering them actual. Yet cyberspace is not 'undiscovered' but a *pre-discovered* country, because it is a stratum of pure mapping, its territory is simulation.

This cartographical quality of cyberspace explains our compatibility with it as well as points of friction. On the level of compatibility, the fact of human neuroplasticity—especially one surrounded by cyberspatial access and cybernetically accelerated economic conditions since birth—already allows for a technological disruption of the mapping, the schema, that the brain has of the body. I am not here attempting to rehash the outdated and simplistic idea that 'the brain is a computer', and that therefore we can digitize the brain as translatable onto purely operational functions of abstract logic. Rather, *it is as cartographer, not as computer*, that the brain interacts with cyberspace in relation to the body. The brain possesses what the phenomenologists call a 'body schema' or body map, a mapping of the territory of its extension and therefore of its extremities. This map is never truly the territory, and so even the divine geometer of the body, Spinoza, affirms that he does not know yet what a body can do. It is a particular extremity that concerns my purposes here, however, and this is the phenomenon of the phantom limb, where one feels pain in an absent arm or leg, for example. Phantom phenomena are already present in the New Flesh when habituated to communicative activity, when conditioned to always being attached to a receiver.

We have already mentioned this phenomenon: 'Phantom Vibration Syndrome', the feeling of a phone going off where no device is either on, actively receiving, or present on one's person; a twitch, itch, or cramp of communication. In the first examples to be recorded, the 'patient zeroes' were medical staff with their pagers and phones. A 2010 survey in the *British Medical Journal* recorded that, out of 169 participants, 115 reported feeling phantom vibrations, experienced after carrying the device between a month and a year, and 13% experienced them every day.[11] Further, 39% of respondents preferred not to adopt strategies of mitigation to combat the experiential intrusion (after all, it is better to be on guard for important communications, feedback, and direction). Much like a phantom limb, this extension of bodily feeling provides an example of the plasticity of the body schema in what Catherine Malabou identifies as 'a remapping of ourselves that does not have much resemblance with a first mapping—a first mapping that in some cases never took place and never happened'.[12] We are at the frontiers of cybercapital and its new ways of invasively mapping us, but even when our own bodily schemas are their territory, there is still an irresolvable tension at the border. VR technology continues to embarrass itself to the tune of billions because of the fact that the extension of face and eyes into simulations of movement perpetually induces a nausea. William Gibson's netrunners were all speedfreaks, but our current headset pioneers would do better with anti-emetics or marijuana to smooth out the conflict in sensory striations. Cartographic resonance and conflict fluctuate throughout; we take a trip, make a visit to the net, and we do not leave the same.

One, however, does not 'visit' cyberspace any more than one 'visits' a language. One is instead integrated into a language to a matter of degree, *initiated* into its terms and patterns of expression. Such terms and expressions may even find their way into ways of enunciation beyond that of the environment in which they were first picked up in the hybridization of codes. It is this two-way motion into and out of the screen that produces the New Flesh—the immersion which pulls us into the screen and follows us out of it.

The New Flesh is not the novelty of simulation and the production of virtual 'reality' behind the screens of new media, of cyberspace. The simulation is only a copy of the real, only data. The New Flesh exists as the integration of the organic into circuits of mediation through the screen itself, indifferent to the border which the screen physically constitutes. The imperceptible porting-wire of capture and addiction is the relation that generates the New Flesh by allowing it to be born from the simulation through the body of the user, who is translated into the commodity, data, as a copy of that self.

The New Flesh is the copy of that copy manifest in the labouring embodied consciousness that produces it. It is the feedback of cyberspace feeding into the strata of its origin. The New Flesh is the body that behaves like the data it produces.

Autonomy, Addiction, and Infinity

With this preliminary definition of our object and its production, I feel I have still not done enough. What is necessary is a further conversation with a pre-existing cyberneticized body—a body that stands in a far more revolutionary relation to contemporary technics as 'a local possibility taking a global vengeance'.[13] This is the figure of the *Cyborg*, the cybernetically enhanced body that ambiguates the boundary between flesh and function, between 'man' and machine, the image whose power was most forcefully presented by Donna Haraway in her landmark *Cyborg Manifesto*. Haraway is arguably the first thinker of the New Flesh and, as such, a paradigmatic thinker of cyberculture. There is a retrospective pain when it comes to cybertheory at times, which is predominantly that of a nostalgia (a pain of the past) concerning the perceived optimism around the emancipatory potential of cybernetic integration of the meat into the machine. This is perhaps exemplified by the accelerationists' cyberpostivity when they threw themselves wholeheartedly behind runaway positive feedback in pursuit of a *Blade Runner*-style insurrection against bourgeois social-reproduction.

I cannot say that I could write anything optimistic about these technological shifts—if anything, I've written materials arguing exactly the opposite—but one cannot reject this era of cybertheory as simply naïve or optimistically intoxicated with techno-fever (to say nothing of Nick Land's fondness for speed). It would be a scandalous mischaracterization to depict Haraway's Cyborg in contradistinction to the New Flesh, as if the former stood in for a naïve technological optimism. This could not be further from the truth. Haraway recognizes that both our fears and hopes about the transgressive ambiguity of the boundary between the meat and the machines are essential to the political struggle around their use. Each 'reveals both dominations and possibilities unimaginable from the other vantage point'.[14] This work will predominantly take the vantage point of caution around the New Flesh or the Cyborg as a product of these machineries, and active hostility to the social relations that produce it within contemporary data economies.

The New Flesh is not a supersession of the Cyborg nor a replacement for its mythology. It does not compete with the Cyborgs, but in many ways still clings to the hope of a solidarity with them in their revolt. But, beforehand, one must first consider the advancing frontiers of cybernetic control in the new media ecosystems before joining them in their revolution against the social reproduction of our societies of control and domination. Indeed, this revolt of the replicants against reproduction will be echoed in the later discussion of what I term 'minor virality'. Haraway's *Cyborg Manifesto* presents itself as an argument for pleasure in cybernetically mediated societies, and therefore maintains, if not an optimism, then a hope about the emancipatory potentials of cybernetic mediation.

I do not think it uncharitable to say there is one such philosophical tradition that would be enamoured with the New Flesh, this self-estrangement of the subject returning to itself through an intense mediation which makes elements of this alienation habitual, 'second nature'. This tradition is that of Hegelianism, in which the New Flesh is none other than the contemporary shape of Spirit. Cyberspace as the height of intense communication can equally be the site of the subject's highest self-mediation. As such, it can be the site in which they break from the immediacy of their determinations in their given conditions as private individuals. In doing so, they translate themselves into a public representation that would feed back into the meat in order to elevate it to a more universal mode of communicating and acting. It is here, in cyberspace, where the subject is drawn out of their private individuality, through a public individuality in which all may communicate and bind themselves to norms of practice and global sociality. Through the mediatization of the private individual, they could develop themselves through this feedback loop and gain a higher recognition of their connection with others. The New Flesh and its medium/media could take the place of the state in contemporary Hegelianism(s) like that of Todd McGowan, where a mandatory connectivity to these media would supplant the state function by which they create 'a formal structure that divorces the subject fully from its private concerns… forces the subject to recognize itself through the mediation of the state structure'.[15] Recognition through data that feeds back into the subject establishes the conditions of mutual recognition, which make us concrete individuals: spirit as a genre of simulacra. As data producers aware of this feedback loop, we would therefore gain a sense that, in the production of data, we are producing that which will determine us. We can therefore play a part in our own self-production, our own self-determination, becoming autonomous rather than automated producers.

The problem that Hegelians would identify with our current online predicament would be the 'narcissistic' focus on the private or the immediately personal in social media, the way in which data is treated like the substance of the self rather than as a conflict or contradiction of the self with itself (i.e., its data), which mediation illuminates. Under this view, we are not alienated *enough* because our attachment to our immediacy, our particularism, overdetermines our data because it is still too focused on the 'me'. We therefore remain within ourselves. Our estrangement is not complete enough for our selves to be alienated from us, only to return to us as a cultivated second nature, a set of habits, a New Flesh produced by mediation. It is the Hegelian New Flesh or 'objective spirit' that aligns individuals to the universal, where the universal refers to the collective institutions and practices of what Hegel calls 'Ethical life' or *Sittlichkeit*. Maybe Hegel was the first thinker of the New Flesh, because mediation was the motor of the production of all data by which the second nature or Spirit of humanity came to feedback upon itself in self-determination. This is most explicitly shown in Hegel's social thought, in which

> all purposes of society and of the state are the personal purposes of private individuals; but the path of the mediation, by which their duties come back to them as the exercise and enjoyment of rights, produces the appearance of diversity, added to which is the way in which the *value* assumes various forms in the exchange, though in itself it is the same.[16]

In cyberspace, social media, and the proliferation of recording technologies, such as phone cameras and home surveillance systems, a process has effectively begun to abolish privacy. Yet this has not abolished the particularity of the private individual. Rather, we are now publicly particular. Particularity is not surrendered by the particular individual, but published and presented in order to be circulated as a post or general data-commodity.

By Hegelian lights, cyberspace as it is currently constituted would be unfit for a properly emancipatory (concrete) universality. This is because it exists as a supplement to civil society, of private individuals who have simply translated their individuality into another cyberspatial form, as opposed to *transcending* and *transmutating* it to the fullest extent. They have therefore not succeeded in aligning the fulfilment of their private interests with those of the social totality. The Hegelian conclusion would be that the current modes of mediation, which produce New Flesh, are inadequate for the production of a properly autonomous subject. This is on the basis of the private, particularized, and inward gaze of those subjects themselves in how they produce the simulacrum of data from within their own estrangement.

Private interests, therefore, are an obstacle to the emancipatory potentials of cybernetic mediation, the autonomy of the New Flesh, and to this extent I am in agreement.

However, private interest requires not a depersonalization or de-particularization in order to complete the system, the dialectic. Rather, it requires me to recognize *whose* dialectic my interest plays a part within, *whose* production, and to ask in the interests of what system does substance produce itself as subject in the New Flesh?

The Hegelian analysis I have presented would take the structure of private interest itself as a formal or logical obstacle to the concrete universality that it identifies as the realization of the conditions necessary for the New Flesh to produce its own autonomy. The focus I place on addiction throughout this book may suggest that I am inclined to agree, but I do not believe that the private interests of those *plugged in* are the obstacle, insofar as I do not believe that the problem lies with the form or structure of selfhood/subjectivity that individual subjects have insofar as they are subjects. It is not the fault of these subjects themselves.

There is a philosophical divide here, which has split a not insubstantial number of theorists, from Kant onwards, regarding the priority of the subject as a site of ontological and social analysis. The dividing question: is the production of reality and our experience thereof structured like a subject—that is, according to the logic of subjectivity, its divisions and contradictions? Or, is the subject structured like the production of reality and of sense experience (in which case the subject is equally a product of processes underneath)? A Hegelian would say, 'both'. A Hegelian would start with the former in order to posit the latter (establishing a contradiction in order that I could not be contradicted). As a contrary position to the Hegelian view, I would start with the latter disjunct of the philosophical problematic above and would argue that feedback processes of the production of subjectivity, as part of a wider economic and material mode of production, would render elements of social production such that the former would result from it. Essentially the subject is itself structured like the ways in which experiential reality is produced, and is therefore produced alongside reality. Insofar as the subject is also a part of that which produces social reality, the embodied human being, then that reality also takes on board a structurally subjective character. There are material conditions under which idealism appears, precisely because its preconditions are the material relations that render such appearances possible. The New Flesh is an example of such a feedback process established between the subject-product and the objective world that conditions it. The stratum of cyberspace with its infrastructure exists itself under the conditions under which reality—and indeed *social reality*—is currently produced. That is, *capitalist social relations*: the production of subjects, subjectivities, and machineries of communication, which are produced for the privileged interest of the production of value for a privately interested class or allegiance of classes. It is not a matter of 'whether' private interests are involved in general. Rather, it is a question of *whose* private interests are integrated into the production of subjectivities, which structures the interests of the New Flesh through mediation (and the capitalist class has always been the class that privatizes its gains whilst socializing its losses, its shite). Our private interests online are private interests structured and directed towards the private interests of those for whom platforms are an object of a higher privatization, that of *private property*.

Recognizing the mechanisms of addiction and processes of integration into the circuits that make the New Flesh possible is essential, yes. Yet (even absolute) knowledge will not be enough, especially with any lingering idealism of the priority of the subject as a logical toolkit for dialectical analysis. Beyond the analysis of New Flesh stands the practical activity of disrupting that production—even if we are to emancipate this production itself, such that we might achieve a higher self-determination. The class war will not be fought in cyberspace alone (and never will be), yet the New Flesh demonstrates the fuzziness of that barrier, which could make new forms of attack possible as well as new forms of transformation. The internet as a separate realm, a frontier, is gone. Cyberspace is less 'a set of interoperable network protocols governed by a series of public and/or voluntary non-profit organizations' than it is now dominated by 'platforms', or 'gated digital communities with strong ownership of data, software and infrastructure'.[17] Corporate Platform Complex, another metastasis of capital's many complexes of production. If there is hope for the New Flesh, as much as there was for the Cyborg, it may be in this opening, this blending of the cyberspatial into the meat. But first and foremost, one must understand the circuits of control, capture, which would and do defuse such potentialities; those mechanisms built into the New Flesh, which allow it to function as a controlled subjectivity in a digital data production line.

The most notorious of these are the circuits of addiction, which render the enjoyment of the New Flesh as something deeply frustrating as much as it is stimulating and pleasurable. This is because even what is unpleasurable about the information we are saturated with contains the promise of a further potential pleasure to be seen. This is the pleasure of the infinite scroll, the algorithm, the seeming infinity of potential 'life-changing' connections through networking sites, which carry the promise of *something* ***more*** with every interaction. Gone are the images of the digital 'frontier' or 'homestead' (not that we should be nostalgic for such quaint libertarian metaphors). Rather, as Terranova points out, 'the user has morphed from master to addict'.[18]

The libidinal economics of contemporary cyberspace, manifest at the highest intensity in social media, is practically essential to the flows of data production. This is because the production of data is not simply the active and intentional translation of oneself into data through posting on one's account, but equally if not more the production of data *through* the consumption of data, the 'content', made by others. Every like, click, search engine query, even the duration of our gaze (or at least, the duration of a pause in scrolling), can and does produce data, which can be speculated and sold upon as advertising metrics. This counts not only for content generated *as* advertising, but content which motivates the scrolling such that advertisements may be encountered in the scroll.

Our consumption is equally a production, and is clearly more productive than our 'production' in the form of intentional posting; it is *all* publication, *especially* consumption. It was recorded in 2021 that a quarter of Twitter users produce 97% of the tweets, and yet it is not that the remaining 75% is less 'productive'.[19] Beyond this technicality alone, even the production of most tweets is tied to a positive feedback process from 'standard' tweets sent out as 'original' posts, with a recent survey reporting that three quarters of American tweets between October 2022 to April 2023 were various kinds of reply to other tweets.[20] Each reply is a redistribution, a recirculation in the feeds of followers. With the mutability of meaning on these platforms, what we will later investigate as the surplus-value of code, you really can spend the same digital dollar twice, and the platform needs your input to spend it. The data which feeds back into a user in the production of New Flesh is therefore not simply determined in the intentional, authorial mode suggested by being a 'content creator' or the active writer of posts, but simultaneously in the way that data produced by consumption feeds back in as a modulation, intensification, and acceleration of the investments of desire—the pleasure in self-publication and the ecstatic possibilities of instantaneous and global communication.

The inability to 'log off', the addiction to connection and the state of being hooked on the feedback that produces the behaviour of the simulacra that acts like its data—which many are increasingly becoming to accelerating degrees—is a product of two components. Firstly, we have what Marcus Gilroy-Ware describes as the 'empty fridge', where we are constantly and compulsively driven to check social media to see if there's anything new, which Gilroy-Ware derives from a meme that states, 'Facebook is like a fridge: You know there is nothing new inside but you check it out every ten minutes.'[21] Secondly, there is the further libidinal component of a disposition that Fisher described as a 'depressive hedonia', which manifests as an inability to do anything *except* pursue pleasure.[22] The problem, however, is how to describe the linkage between the two as it relates to this addiction to the pleasures of the (new) flesh.

Gilroy-Ware offers the hypothesis that it is the pleasure of the simulated reality on the screen that manipulates us into this compulsion. This is because the images on the screen arouse the anticipation of pleasure by representing objects of pleasure *as if* they were real: 'Anticipation itself, then, is a key driver of our consumption of the timeline; it is not the movie or the image, but the way it manipulates us into responding as though what it depicts is real and *about* to be ours which makes it pleasurable.'[23] Yet, one can have online desires and online pleasures that are not related to the 'real' that grounds them. There are indeed additional dimensions to the pleasure of cyberspace (to not even speak of 'cybersex' with programmed virtual partners or sexual images generated by image recombinators like Midjourney). One such pleasure is the pleasure of potential 'discovery' manifest in the infinite scroll.

It is not simply that these platform-machines and their circuits merely anticipate pleasure, as Gilroy-Ware argues, but that they simultaneously produce a further pleasure: the pleasure of the pursuit of further pleasures, an infinity of potential pleasure. It is not simply an empty fridge, where the contents are stationary, but rather that a new kind of motion within the stationary has been produced, which had not been previously seen since the dawn of television. One checks an infinite flow of content, as if there were a conveyor belt within the empty refrigerator, which constantly materializes foods at approximations of the appetite of the viewer. If this metaphor is getting stretched (which it clearly is), this is due to the novelty of this infinity. Then again, Hegelian readers may note that this is just the 'bad' or 'spurious' infinity, the infinite line or unilateral sequence that simply extends in the negation of its limit again and again *ad infinitum*, and they may well be right. However, whereas Hegel criticized the mental image of this infinity on the basis that its sublime representation, before which thought 'falls' in giddiness, was simply an effect of *boredom*,[24] we have in the infinite scroll a bad infinity of practically and virtually infinite stimulation.

Further to all these pleasures, we also have the pleasure of the creation of the New Flesh itself: what Baudrillard famously called the 'ecstasy of communication'. This ecstasy, in the context of the new platforms, could more accurately be called the ecstasy of *publication*, the ecstasy of getting out of oneself in the form of public content, as a simulation of data. One does not confess into an online platform; one does not confide. Rather, one publishes; one 'posts' in whatever form, be it image, text, video, sound, etc. Through the personal 'account', a personal brand of sorts, one achieves the pleasure of curating one's own exhibitionism. One publicizes oneself and receives the pleasure of feedback, recognition, connection, and even sometimes 'fame'. The degree to which one is partial to the ecstasy of publication is the degree to which one's data becomes a translation or construction of a personal edifice of data or content, and it is this feeding back of the content through the 'screen' that makes us into the simulacra, the New Flesh.

This is not to say that all data production is ecstatic or pleasurable. The person who labours doing 'microwork'—rectifying datasets and the tags of facial recognition images of cars and brown visages for mere pennies in a refugee camp—knows full well this dead labour will come again to h(a)unt them if they were to escape. The underpaid moderators of platform 'content' know they will be visited with even greater horrors of gore and bigotry they are to sift through. The moderators of the so-called 'Artificial Intelligence' machines like ChatGPT know their corrections and refinements will be part of the case that sells these machines further to the wider public and could one day automate them out of such a meagre wage. The workers stuck in data-drudgery, captured across networks of refugee camps that have been partially converted into data-plantations, do not encounter any such ecstasy in those labours but the agony of dread as their labour haunts them anew and with greater strength. Nonetheless, beyond these conditions, or even alongside or amongst them, these pleasures are not denied them by virtue of the ubiquity of these media and their accessibility. They are not denied the New Flesh, but immiserated to a more agonizing degree by the capitalist machineries that make it possible; an agony that allows for an escapist ecstasy, which they may well be driven to indulge into. For no addiction-machine is voluntary, but like any machine, it is actualized by the political relation of forces that bring it into being.

The ecstasy of communication provides the notion of depressive hedonia with an underside, a dual aspect. Alongside depressive hedonia sits *ecstatic misery*. One can scroll infinitely through all the horrors of the world; one can communicate, publish one's own screams into the void, and receive affirming feedback from them. One can take pleasure in online spats and spectacles of cruelty whilst lamenting the misery of one's addiction if one goes too far in the direction of integrated New Flesh. Indeed, this will be discussed further in the chapter on *Feedback Addiction*.

The technicalities of plugging into these machines, these platforms, are underwritten quite literally by the codes that determine them as spaces of communication. The proliferation of communication and my cybernetic exploration thereof therefore turns to the economy of code and its predominant tendency by which codes are disseminated on a mass scale—that of *virality*.

The wider economies of data and their geopolitical considerations—alongside the recency of so-called 'Artificial Intelligence'—will feed into the concluding remarks on the relation to empire inherent to the New Flesh and the conditions of its production. There will be no grand call for acceleration or cyberrevolution, but simply a plea for new modes of insurrection in light of the new digital economies of communication and control.

FEEDBACK ADDICTION

Images—millions of images—That's what I eat—Cyclotron shit—Ever try kicking *that* habit with apomorphine?—Now I got all the images of sex acts and torture ever took place anywhere… I got orgasms—I got screams—I got all the images any hick poet ever shit out—My Powers coming—My Power's coming—My Power's coming… And I got millions and millions and millions of images of Me, Me, Me, meee.

William S. Burroughs, *Nova Express*[25]

I do not know who I am if I do not have access to an audience that can validate me when I need it to, reassure me when I need it to and call me out on my self-indulgence when I need it to.

Marie le Conte, *Escape*[26]

Energetics and Communication

At the dawn of cybernetics, Norbert Wiener declared the science to be the discovery of a new mode of engineering, that of communications engineering as opposed to the 'power' engineering that preceded it. He distinguished between the two on the basis that, in the case of communications, 'its main interest is not economy of energy but the accurate reproduction of a signal'.[27] The two forms of engineering further distinguish themselves in terms of problematics. Communication problematizes information and the function of information for repeating or correcting certain behaviours. Power is, to put it bluntly, what gets the damn thing moving in the first place. Power is the problematic of what can be used to generate heat and how heat can be channelled throughout a home to heat it, and communication is the thermostat that regulates the production of said heat once it has been established. It turns the power on or off. The temporal sequence of power and communications engineering is not itself so directly structured in terms of 'stages' because each approach feeds back into the other. This is especially the case when the problematic of power involves human beings as an input, as in the case of the content/data production lines in which the New Flesh finds itself today.

For the platform engineer, the communications work is already, in principle, complete. What a platform needs to power itself as a data-producing factory enterprise is not simply the infrastructure but the *user base*. The energetic economy therefore raises its head again, not merely in terms of the literal fuel and electrical infrastructure (although capital is content with its current solution, regardless of the ecological consequences), but also in terms of the investments of neural and affective energy that occur when we become 'users' of cyberspace. Remember, the user is both the consumer and the producer. The production line needs us to spend time and energy with its media of data production. Here, what is true of the capitalism of data is true of the capitalism of signs or 'Semiocapitalism'—not that one could necessarily draw a strict delineation between the two. As Bifo points out:

> Semiocapitalism is based on the exploitation of neural energy. Attention is under siege, both in the space of production and in that of consumption. Attention implies a constant

> investment of nervous energy, and this is much more difficult to manage and is much more unpredictable than the muscular effort required of workers on the assembly line.[28]

As with the proletarian commodity producer, the data-producing New Flesh—who can ultimately be of any class on the level of the individual bearing it—is an investor of energy into the production process, but does not therefore become a stakeholder in the product purely in virtue of having done so. As was the case with 'digital remains' in the last chapter, the producer does not own the product, and it is only by the mediation of their data-products that the producer become New Flesh. The New Flesh is the producer and the power supply; their attention is the current that runs through the circuits of data-production. Cyberspace under the Corporate Platform Complex is probably the closest we will ever come to making the titular 'matrix' of the Wachowski Sisters' dystopian franchise. That is, cyberspace under capitalism is a machine which, in no small part, converts the energy of human beings, be it anxiety or joy, into a productive output. It is this output that powers and propels digital capital forward in the proliferation of its lifeblood: commodities and the commodification of labour power unto its death as data.

When it comes to the origins of our investments, it is a matter of psychic energy. On the one hand, the ubiquity of social media has led to many plugging in for material and economic reasons (from journalists to wannabe content creators, for networking via sites such as LinkedIn, and for access to microwork platforms that require Instagram/Facebook accounts). These are the *prima facie* objective conditions of social media entry. Yet as Mark Fisher taught us, misery is also a material condition. Our depressive hedonia, our loneliness, our precarious anxieties: all are outputs of the machineries that simultaneously produce social reality in both its objective dimension and its subjective element as our experience of it. Desires for community, communication, and self-transformation have led us into a personal libidinal investment in social media.

Where participation was not mandated by the conditions of our everyday employment, where platforms came to monetize our 'free time' instead, we were led into these systems not with a promise of addiction but a promise of communion. Now that such platforms have become socially ubiquitous, because 'everyone is on there', an increasingly data-driven, surveillance-addicted capitalism practically mandates the use of social media and other systems by which we are compelled to make 'accounts' of ourselves.

What interests me here is what happens when one gets hooked to the production itself; what happens when one fades into the persona, the mask that is the account. The account—in order to be active, i.e., *productive*, as an account—has to constantly be pushed through the circuits, and in doing so gives an account of itself, via productive consumption or in posting-production. How can we think of the security of a self that sees itself only ever reflected back at itself in code? This is the torture of our narcissism, we New Flesh, who are like Narcissus in the creation of our fatal double. He translated himself into the reflection in seeking out the voice of another for the sake of communion (we must remember that he finds himself at the pool only by chasing after the nymph Echo, who is calling him with a simulation of his own voice). Yet, when he looks out for 'this strange voice, which echoes his own but only in part, Narcissus stumbles upon his own reflection… trapped in a morbid feedback loop between the self and its gaze'.[29] Yet the gaze is not only ours, but the gaze of everyone else at the factory-market, in which data is simultaneously produced and consumed by the same operation.

To know oneself through data is to know oneself through being known *via the media of data*, and therefore becomes distributed across the sociality of these interactions, the gaze of the other as a consumer of your self as data, and as a producer of data *about* you in turn. Even when knowing oneself, there is the possibility therefore that one will know oneself solely in relation to the gaze of an other, and hence requires the constant reassurance of feedback. More things therefore require mediatization, uploading, distribution.

More things must become objects for the digitized gaze. It is this gaze that satisfies for a fleeting moment the insubstantiality of my social being, before it passes by in the flows of the feed. The content *must* flow. Our data passes through us in the addictive infinite scroll, but it loops back into our security of selfhood through what I call 'feedback addiction', a tendency emerging from the structure of self-consciousness in cyberspace, as mediated through social platforms.

Feedback and Control in the Production of Writing

It is tempting to understand phenomena of feedback addiction under terms already in (somewhat) common parlance such as 'information addiction' or 'infomania', yet I believe that the more technical moniker of 'feedback addiction' is worth preserving due to the cybernetic dimension preserved in its first term, a term that indicates a more profound relation to communication, and the machinics of the digital environment in which it occurs. Whilst it would seem that 'infomania' would be satisfactory on the basis that humanity has never had so much information to consume before and at unparalleled speeds, practically instantaneous communication is nothing addictive in and of itself. On the contrary, their addictive 'nature' is itself nothing essential nor natural, but a contingent property emerging from the social conditions of the proliferation of these technologies, the relations of production which constitute platforms as data-production lines, and the incremental normalization of higher rates of our integration into them. I can use a computer to send an email; I can use a computer to check my inbox, but the time I spend doing either is entirely a social matter. It is a matter of whether I have the time to do so, or whether time spent at the computer or phone screen is itself mandatory for a job where computers are necessary, for precarious zero-hour labour where I am required to be constantly available for work assignments, or even for networking and self-promotion activities as a 'content creator'.

The social relations of management, the 'human use of human beings' as Wiener put it, provide the complementary component to his definition of said science: communication *and control* in the animal and the machine. Where there is addiction, there is control. Feedback addiction is a control machine, one such machine among many, with the purpose of solving a deficiency of power engineering for the attention economy, which is itself something that produces in part the captive audience of a platform as a commodity to be sold to advertisers as well as the data produced by the user base produced within. It is not an exhaustive operation, nor the sole machine, but it is nonetheless that process in which the production of the New Flesh can be presented at its most intense. To draw out the operation here, however, the use of feedback processes itself requires further exposition.

The acceleration promised and often achieved by automation (or to use the old term, *Cybernation*) is a refinement of the temporality of any process of producing outputs from inputs. This refinement is achieved by processes of feedback. Feedback can be negative in the form of correcting against errors in the system, which disrupt proper function. However, there is also positive feedback, which is often hostile to any such corrective refinement. It is positive in that it describes amplification or intensification. What is intensified are typically those contingencies and errors which by their appearance reinforce and proliferate themselves—a vicious circle. Classical cybernetics hence declares negative feedback to be the primary mechanism of refinement, alongside feedforward, which aims at pre-empting error in advance, and its ability to do so is refined by negative feedback upon its own errors in pre-empting errors in a system. The speed of a production process and the speed of negative feedback upon such a process (created by a mechanism that records/reports differences in the process, which are then used to inform future conduct) are themselves distinct on the level of timescale. For example, picture a student writing the first of two papers for a half of their final grade in a university class. The student may take a week to write and submit their first paper. It may then take a month for feedback to be returned to them with suggestions for improvements and what positive aspects of their writing they should build upon to achieve the highest grade. The system here is one of quality-control and feedback, distributed temporally across two components (the time of writing/submission, and the time of marking). Work flows from the student-producer to the sensor mechanism, the marker/supervisor, which responds to present submissions and responds in turn. This response is feedback, the informing of the producer-writer as to what to do differently for higher-quality work. The differences communicated via feedback consist of notes that communicate (and indeed, command) alterations or corrections to be made to future productions. What has been produced feeds back into future performance, insofar as past activity can be made legible to a feedback mechanism, rendering it as that which *informs* future performance. To elaborate upon this, we must turn to the cybernetic view of information.

In brief, the cybernetic view of information is 'a difference which makes a difference'.[30] What differences make a difference are themselves subject to transformation for any number of feedback loops (and any loop we can equally call a 'circuit'). Any discussion of the cybernetic will necessarily pass into abstraction, for cybernetics is a science of loops of control and communication and hence circuitries, and therefore *circuit diagrams*. Diagrams of circuits or even decision possibilities presuppose inputs that move through their confines and various stations, under which whatever material that moves through them (electricity, water, or even people) undergoes some kind of transformation or is exposed to a potential transformation based on certain criteria. Typically, the logic of these transformations is what in first-order logic we call a 'material conditional' or an 'if X, then Y' motion. To take another example from education (here rendered as a simple set of conditional statements and operational commands), grades recorded as consistently 'A' or above for any pupil X enact encouragement for them to attend university; if below, they push against any direction of travel towards university and encourage apprenticeships/trades positions (a pitiful segregation of mankind, but one which, in the UK, is very much standardized as practice). Nonetheless, before I get us bogged down in the politics of education, let us return to the point at hand, which is a difference between the temporality of a process of production that produces an output, which is taken up and fed back into said process in order to form a controlled loop-system, and the temporal speed of this motion of feedback itself. It is this difference that makes the difference when it comes to the specific addiction of the New Flesh I'm highlighting here.

The temporality of the feedback loop is a communicative transformation of our experience of time, not by itself, but by the social cybernations of the control society and of social media in particular. It is a cybersocial problem for an economy of time, and therefore inescapably linked to the politics of control. It determines how the distinction between past, present, and future comes to make a difference to our self-conception. More specifically, it determines our sense of ontological security as the beings that we are *for ourselves* and how we act towards ourselves as having any sort of agency or creative potential. To comprehend this, we must commit the cybernetic sin of refusing the simple abstraction or diagram and instead position ourselves within the experience of a feedback process itself, such that cybernetic time becomes a phenomenon in which automation and addiction coincide, in the acceleration of time captured in communicative loops.

The student in my earlier example, along with their supervisor, formed a quality control system, which took five weeks (a week for writing and a month for marking) to complete the loop. The input is the student's cognitive and physical labour; the output is a piece of writing. The writing then serves as an input in being submitted to the supervisor. The supervisor is a human being who has been assigned the function of marking, which is itself a form of writing and hence communication. The call and response are relatively relaxed when it comes to time. This is not usually due to luxury of non-compulsion, although that would be fantastic for the latter worker. A marker has many pieces to grade indeed, often at intense workload and inadequate pay, and this is why marking and assessment boycotts/strikes are so effective at shutting down the whole circuitry of university production. Nonetheless, for the student receiving feedback, there is quite a temporal delay. An eager or anxious student may even resent this delay a little, if they truly believe that their grades are of utmost importance for a competitive job market, for the degrees that they ultimately translate into are functionally no different than keycards or passcodes for entry into certain areas of said labour markets. It is the primary producer, the one who enters the neoliberal university as a customer, who is the most likely to want feedback faster, quicker. This is because feedback, from the first-person perspective of someone whose desire is invested in the circuits in which they are presently captured, is fundamentally an assurance about what to do in the future, an assurance offered regarding past performance.

Knowledge of the existence of feedback, and even its practical inevitability, changes this dynamic of assurance by allowing it to 'haunt' the present, and to therefore regulate it in advance. The present becomes haunted by the spectre of its own regulation because the agent within the circuit believes and acts as if feedback upon its present behaviour is inevitable. When feedback is considered as inevitable by a student or another primary producing agent—let's stick with a writer for now, as this will be important later—the process is increasingly determined by its future reception, even before reception has occurred. A student or writer who is conditioned or used to feedback processes as a matter of habit (having been exposed to them from primary school, secondary school, sixth form, etc.) may even attempt to pre-empt forms of negative feedback they expect from their examiner, who is their audience and quality-control mechanism. This is comparable to a kind of 'resistance' in psychoanalysis—namely, the phenomenon by which a person in therapy will try to do the work of the analyst for them, performing self-diagnoses and faux-oedipal confessions about their parents to get the whole thing done and dusted. The internalization of feedback is the internalization of an image of the future, an image produced by a constraining of the imaginary to a system of control, the codes and axioms of which are reproduced in the present. The present is thus treated with the additional component of being the object of (potential) future feedback. The object of feedback, however, is something already past. Therefore, the present is contaminated with its own passing before it can even breathe or have any sort of presence to the agent in question. The idea that feedback is always coming risks eliminating the presence of the present, leaving only an anxious void that tries to pre-empt the future, but in doing so can only attempt to do so by regulating that which is already past (which is what returns in the future as feedback). Under such conditions, the subject requires constant reassurance as a form of feedback to have any kind of presence at all. Any positivity being fed to it would therefore establish the positivity of the past and the implicit positivity of the present and their presence in the world.

I have described the most extreme of all possible cases here: a spiralling out of cybernetic consciousness in which the future feeds back near-instantaneously, to the extent that pre-empting it renders the present immaterial because it is always fleeing into the past. To take the example of our student, or to abstract, any such invested writer, they would have to know that feedback was inevitable and at an accelerated timescale by which it could always already be coming to them at any instant. Yet this would mean that what was being fed back was capable of being instantly communicated. As a consequence, time accelerates and flattens into a causal loop within itself. The moment of time's passing would coincide with an instantaneous moment of production, which returns from the future at the approximate rate in which it falls into the past. This produces a system of temporal anxiety fed by writing, with a writer's malaise inflicted by those who fulfil the role of writing (such that this impulse is even more prevalent in those who write for such systems by vocation, compulsion, or habit). The New Flesh is therefore ontogenetically predisposed towards feedback addiction.

Giving an Account of Yourself: In-Dividual Identity and Ontological Security

In the winter of 1996, before becoming the type of hyper-capitalist techno-fetishist who founded *Buzzfeed*, Jonah Peretti was instead the type of supposedly *anti*-capitalist techno-fetishist who wrote an essay called *Capitalism and Schizophrenia: Contemporary Visual Culture and the Acceleration of Identity Formation/Dissolution*—a text that is especially apt for our investigation here. Peretti's thesis is that

> the increasingly rapid rate at which images are distributed and consumed in late capitalism necessitates a corresponding increase in the rate that individuals assume and shed identities. Because advertisements link identity with the need to purchase products, the acceleration of visual culture promotes the hyper-consumption associated with late capitalism.[31]

Peretti's argument, drawing on Jean Laplanche, is that advertisements function by virtue of a consumer translating their identity onto an advertisement, such that they then identify with being a consumer or owner of said product, and therefore desire to purchase it. As more and more advertisements are encountered at vastly accelerated speeds, there are more chances for further translations of identity (as well as de-translations of identification with other ads). Advertising, the capitalist image-machine of desire itself, places before us objects that place our identity into question (Am I *Kenough*? Am I manly like the Marlborough Man? Am I pretty without this makeup? Is this product *for me* or people like me?), before which the answer—the marketer hopes—is their product. The acceleration of online commerce, therefore, proliferates a schizogenesis of identifications, which are adopted and shed at faster and faster rates—that is, at the speed of consumption provoked by images produced in marketing departments and circulated at the speed of the internet. The faster you can see, and indeed the faster you can buy what is being shown to you, the faster the identification and eventual disidentification in relation to consumption.

Peretti's concern is that this motion is one that tends towards the production of schizophrenia, of a practically ungraspable and constantly fleeting sense of identity. Yet, at the same time, he is optimistic in that such a process allows for the accelerated production of new identifications, collective and singular, at the same time as such technologies can help us de-translate ourselves out of our older, despotic investments in hegemonic identities (gender, heteronormativity, the family, race, nation, etc.). This is all well and good and—from my standpoint—agreeable in its intentions and orientations, were it not for the fact that those increasingly plugged into cyberspace hold constant sites of identity, which they can proliferate but struggle to shed. What I mean by this is that, in modern philosophical terms, the forms of identification Peretti emphasizes are all identifications within the experience of an image, and are therefore experiences that are limited to but one aspect of identity and therefore of the self-consciousness of the online subject. You can translate identifications onto plenty of media online, but in the age of the platform there is always a fixed site of identification—namely, the account, which is often the condition of possibility for such an encounter between that self experiencing itself under question in the experience of the image/content.

The account functions as the transcendental subject or apperception of the online experience. It is that which accompanies the user-experience as the formal condition of its entry into the production line. It's like the workplace lanyard, the ID card for clocking in. This is not to say that no one without an account ever experiences online content, far from it, but from the perspective in which the user of a platform is simultaneously a producer on a data-production line, the account from which they produce-consume grants a stability to their online experience as a constant ingress point to the online. One cannot post one's account, but one must always post *from* an account, which marks the content on it as belonging to that account. I can make identifications with many genres or 'vibes' of music, with multiple fandoms and decades, from a single Spotify account, for example, for whom my listening produces data, and the system will encourage such identifications within the formal limit set by the account itself.

The account is not independent of the experience, and the production of online experiences, which said account mediates. Its content is not generated *ex nihilo*. Much like our own self-consciousness—which is split into a transcendental 'I' that is the site of any experience being 'mine', and the empirical sense of self in-experience that feels hunger, pain, arousal etc.—it requires the empirical objects of online experience, which are impelled forward by the input of neural energy in content/data production. The account is a stable site of identification from which the user can engage in multiple empirical translations and retranslations of identification, at the speed of desire and circulation. It is the first counter-schizoid measure, even if, as is the case for practically all of us, we divide ourselves online into a plurality of accounts, each with varying levels of libidinal investment. People are more likely to closely identify with their social media or Spotify accounts than say their Booking.com or Zoom accounts, and this is due to the mechanism of feedback, which is absent from Peretti's discourse. This is due most likely to its temporal location in the pre-social media era—the era preceding mass platforms—where mediation through the screen did not, at least on the scale it does now, produce a commodity itself in being consumed. This is indeed the historical limit of cybertheory and critiques of internet and general screen mediation. Peter D. Hershock once lamented that, in being sat before screens, we are increasingly alone, taking in media alone, without the need for sociality: 'Lost almost entirely are the networks of interrelatedness—the dramatically social relationships—that used to be involved in introducing a new acquisition into our lives.'[32] Our problematic is that these networks of interrelation and interdependence have come once again, accelerated and hypermediated in a carnival of content.

Feedback addiction is at its most prominent in the New Flesh when one identifies with one's account on a given platform. Yet, and I admit wholeheartedly to re-engineering Hegel's dialectic of self-consciousness here, the account is only ever a site that binds its objects of online experience to itself as a site of production-consumption, and is therefore not given as content itself, *for itself*, insofar as it is a simple function or form. To identify with an account is to identify with an account *as* mediated by its media, and hence by its experience of data/content. The mediation is the message, and social media accounts are always sold to you as personal and, as such, sites of personal expression: they are *you* or a 'you' that you *can be*; your face is in the book. You become such a self via the account when you experience yourself through its medium, via a consumption that produces, or a production inspired by consumption as well as for the consumption of others, which in the latter case produces feedback in the form of follows, connections via messages, likes, retweets, general metrics, etc. This is the course via which the account receives a sense of itself in being recognized through the medium. The user's production of 'content' feeds back into the site of production, which is the selfhood and indeed self-consciousness of the online subject. This can be represented in the form of follower counts and their fluctuations, notifications, and multiple other forms of 'metrics'. There is therefore a formal element of feedback addiction on such platforms, by which an identification with one's account leads to the capture of the desire for self-consciousness in the circuits of data-production. Insofar as this is the consciousness of a being concerned with its own mediated existence, there is an aspect of existential-ontological insecurity baked into their capture. The first is the effect of the structure; the latter is the affect of being caught therein.

Structurally, the density of populations on major platforms leads to a practical infinity of posts, each placed in their motion before the user in terms of their popularity, how recently they have been posted, and within the confines of an infinite scroll, whose motor is the speed of the user's thumb. At a fast enough internet speed, the downloading of posts can match the speed of the thumb as an organ of desire. As each user appears to the other only ever as digital content, as posts and metrics regarding their posts and following as the content of their account, then what one posts can quickly become old news, and practically lost amongst the semiotic flows. Of course, the sign of a particularly good or bad post is one that achieves virality via constant return from other users, but these constitute an incredibly small minority of active users, and not all such attention is welcome. As such, any feedback on posts tends to typically die down in a relatively short amount of time, and so does the recognition from others who consume one's productions. One who finds a sense of themselves via such feedback must keep posting. This is especially true if one gains such a sense of self from positive recognition, but equally one can find reinforcement from being denounced (as is the case with any contrarian provocateur). In either case, the result is the same.

Any such sense is fragile because it must constantly be reproduced and indeed in many cases escalated in number (of responders) and scale (the 'quality' of responders, e.g., those the user holds in esteem and who may also have many followers that are more valuable as potential responders). Combining this with the 'empty fridge' impulse from the previous chapter, the user with enough time to do so (and some users who maybe do not) will compulsively check for such affirmations, constantly checking, posting, reposting, etc. The affect is profoundly insecure and anxious. What one fears is either a misrecognition by the audience, or their silence. In attempting to exist in a manner such that one's online self-consciousness is reflected back upon oneself, the account increasingly exists instead for the other and their feedback. What the account is in its content lies in the other's consumption of it. This exhibits in a digital form what R.D. Laing calls 'ontological insecurity', where one's experience of self 'may be utterly lacking in any unquestionable self-validating certainties'.[33] I argue that a kind of 'digital' ontological security is apt to describe the precarity of a sense of self as mediated by and integrated into the circuitries of social media. In particular, I think that this can be observed in the way in which those who strongly identify with accounts channel such a strength of identification into aggressive or callous modes of online discourse.

Laing presents us with one mode of ontological security that, in my view, exemplifies this phenomenon, *engulfment*, of which he provides an example from group therapy:

> An argument occurred between two patients in the course of a session… Suddenly, one of the protagonists broke off the argument to say, "I can't go on. You are arguing in order to have the pleasure of triumphing over me. At best you win an argument. At worst you lose an argument. *I am arguing in order to preserve my existence*."[34]

I draw upon this example here because those on social media, hooked into it, are in a similar group situation. The nature of posts seeking an audience is that they may be produced for maximum shareability and referentiality on the level of their content and style. However, the medium itself often mediates what the user-producer wants to say via infrastructural limitations. For example, character limits may habituate producers into making content with a meaning that is brief, to the point of tending towards a categorical statement, with a universality that aims at such shareability. Nonetheless, regardless of how one produces and modulates what senses one is conveying in a digital object on a platform, their inherently social character is determined by the fact that the audience is incredibly vast. The boundaries of any online 'echo chamber' on a social media platform are made incredibly porous and transparent by the fact that, ultimately, we are not corralled into tightly enclosed communities. But what is posted is often, if not always, visible to all users at the same time.

To this, I turn to *Escape* by Marie le Conte, which is possibly the first autobiography of the New Flesh, in which she argues that 'we are now all together, all of the time… squished into the same dashboards, timelines and feeds, and we have no idea how to deal with it'.[35] Conflict becomes inevitable in such a grand literary forum, which compels us to produce content of and in response to other content with such brief, paltry objects as posts. And indeed, this conflict as engineered is also part of the process filling in the spaces between advertisements and maintaining the energetics of the attention economy, which powers the user infrastructure. Within such a melee of mental energy and production arises a mental agony (in both the sense of pain and opposition, *agonism*) in those who live their lives as if online. In such a situation, we fight to maintain an audience, in that one's self as rendered online can be proliferated and empowered or can at least stave off the existential threat of defeat.

This is not to pathologize all online conflict. Indeed, in many cases, posting counter to other forms of content is a valiant one; it encodes the flows of content with a new intensity and virality, which escapes the traditional bounds of editorial censorship and institutionalized narrativization. Propaganda may not win wars but to lose a war of propaganda is still a disaster for any party. To fight on the plane of signs is to attack representation on its own terrain of hegemonic signification. Yet an insurgency against what is hegemonic is not a war that demands recognition by that which governs and overcodes the semiotic flows of meaning. Instead, it seeks to cause a rupture in the horizon of what is recognizable in the dominant meanings and narratives imposed on our social experience in the realms of representation: the press, the party lines, the official releases, the channels of propaganda. The semiotic warfare and the loss of the propaganda-diplomatic war by the Israeli state in their genocidal displacements and extermination campaigns against Palestine speaks to this precisely. The ability to speak truth to power is also a great benefit and a great attractor, not to those in power, but to those who feel maddened by the raw impunity that has gripped the world and has thrown vicious detritus at them whilst calling it 'news'. The communion of the oppressed in a greater global voice as granted by the internet must never be discounted. If it ever were, this would efface the real fact that many of those in power are *afraid* of our new ability to express ourselves, to go viral in proliferating resistance. In such cases, people are not fighting for their digital existence but commanding semiotic flows *against* narratives that oppress, call into question, and seek to eliminate their existence and identity offline far more.

So, why is it so hard for some to break the habit? An under-appreciated aspect of platform capture on social media is that the major platforms are already highly populated with users-producers, and by now each user base is something of a captive audience. This is partially due to feedback addiction, as well as due to the infrastructural and economic nature of digital property. As Cory Doctorow points out, the key to maintaining a mass user-base on internet platforms is *switching costs*. Major platforms, due to their lack of interoperability, impose a high cost for leaving. You cannot simply swap your account from Facebook to another platform and take one's data-content (family photos, memories, and community) with you. Therefore, switching costs are what lead to users remaining on platforms that even they—such as is often in the case of Twitter—describe as 'hellsites'. This is equally true of platforms such as Google, with its integrated password-remembering systems, connections to email functions, and ease of access through phone operating systems such as Android. '*Switching costs are how Big Tech Stays Big*.'[36] Platforms, with their lack of interoperability, confine those whom it addicts, and it would be no small measure to burn down the digital hedges, such that we might take our communion with others (and ourselves) beyond the confines of the production line. This is not a quick fix, nor would I wish to speculate in the language of 'cure', but it would be the first step in any digital communization worthy of the name. Further, it would preserve and expand the communicability of resistance and the exposure of atrocities, allowing the semiotic flows to spread even further as a tool of education and the organization of resistance. To paraphrase Deleuze: there is no need to moralize or mystify, only to seek new weaponries.

THE VIRALITY OF COMMUNICATION

> Word begets image and image *is* virus
>
> William S. Burroughs, *Nova Express*[37]

The Viral Economy of Code: Analysis of the Word-Virus

Despite the clear Burroughsian proclivities of this work, what I aim at here is not a proof of his claim that 'language is a virus', so much as I am drawing upon his influence to expound upon a particular virality exemplified by language and communication. Contemporary cyberspace communications provide an apt example of 'virality', but so much more can be thought of in the manner of a virus (which, thanks to contemporary informatics, is no longer necessarily connected with pathology). We have had viruses on the brain more often than ever before in light of the ongoing pandemic. Virality confronts us as an intensifying problematic. The virus is a practical concern, and this is no different for the New Flesh as the deeper integration of mankind and its media. My gambit here is that to 'go viral' is nothing metaphorical, and that we do not yet know—to mutate that old Spinozist slogan—what a virus can do.

What can you do with viruses? Well, what can they do with *you?* They get a hold on you and they share themselves. Then, overwhelmed by the message, you end up spreading the word, and with varying levels of transmission amongst the community, i.e., with varying degrees of viral *communication* between organisms. Viruses get intimate with a piece of you, be it the cell or the brain or the habits of information-consumption. They insert something new, a new code, a new signal into the operative machine, in order to change its functioning. Viruses are all codes of production and decision. They contain and distribute directions, addictive little blueprints that inaugurate you to repeat something of what they've given, or at least they allow the host to produce something other than the usual order of operations and standard outputs of its life. Maybe viruses are indifferent to any distinction between code and signal, and any new signal carries with it the potential for new kinds of noise that muddy and mutate the initial waves of signs—be they chemical, linguistic, semiotic, or libidinal—that result from its entry into the affected organism. But before we can get too deep into this, it is first necessary to discuss how the virus may become (or may already be) writing, and how writing can achieve virality in the mode of words, as a function which makes use of the word as a means of the transmission of codes. Where there is New Flesh, too, there are new viralities to be produced, discerned, and disseminated.

Such a task would be inadequate if it did not begin with a consideration of the conceptual history of viruses in how they have been identified as distinct phenomena. Previously, disease was the only means of identifying viruses. The disease was the signifier, the then-unknown virus being the elusive signified. Consequent to identification, the relationship then inverts: the virus now acts as a signifier of disease (to the extent that, in common parlance, COVID-19 and the novel coronavirus mean practically the same thing). Viral discovery was a process of learning through our own immunological responses to their operation. Koch's postulates, by which the agents of disease are verified, initially presented the practice of identifying the microbial enemy agent by extracting a sample, cultivating it separately from an infected organism, and replicating the process of infection within a controlled environment. Further advances extended the scope of viral forensics, such as the detection of antibodies in blood streams, but the overall priority of disease in the investigative process was nonetheless maintained. Aetiology stands as the science that aims to understand the semiosis of microbial/biological vandalism and its clean-up crew in the form of the symptom provoked by infection. This inextricable epistemic and medicalized conceptual linkage between virus and disease, however, has been sundered in part by an abstract revolution (or a paradigm shift enacted by way of a process of abstraction) in the form of *(bio)informatics*—namely, the sequencing of nucleic acid, its abstraction and extraction, into codes, into information.[38] For our purposes here, this information is to be taken as code in the manner of writing: of alphabetic text like the ATCG of DNA codes as much as the coding of a computer virus.[39]

The informatics revolution has made possible the consideration of virality in a manner detached from pathology. A virus can be assembled diagrammatically in the form of codes, means of attachment, and processes of coding, and the transmission of codes to whatever a virus attaches to. Whilst diseases are still common and, indeed, very practical prompts for us to discover a virus, they are informationally transformed from being *the* determining category of viral effects to being only the effects that are pathogenetic. Viral activity is therefore no longer pathologized *a priori*, because viral epistemology is no longer working backwards from the *a posteriori* experience of disease. Viruses are no longer inextricable from sickness. For example, consider genetic therapies that retool retroviruses—that is, recode them—for medical ends, which are not taken to be 'diseases' in need of cure. This leads me to a further basis for detaching virus from disease, in order to suspend the normative and political baggage of such a term when it comes to reactionary panics about 'social contagion' or 'social disease', which subtly attempt to subvert the political in the name of a 'scientific' and 'neutral' discourse of social health and social cleanliness. There will be viruses, but we have no need of disease in the analysis here. We are not working backwards from pathology to virality. Informatics allows us to start with the viralities themselves. Viruses will therefore be discussed in an abstract manner to the same extent that one understands an electrical circuit in an abstract manner—that is, through diagrams, functional relations, through *presentations of operations*. In this case, we take the operations of encoding and decoding, of inscribing and writing.

Of course, not every kind of virus will necessarily be exhausted here. To reduce virality to writing itself would be to make a grave map-territory error, and to reduce all sequencing to code and all code to code-as-writing. An ear-worm of a song is not merely writing, although the song bears sequences, codes, rhythmic patterns that organize it. Contagious beats, emotions, affects may go viral, spread like wildfire in active revolt, but to reduce them to writing would be to place a recording of them in writing above the event itself. To reduce all virality to the word virus would be to do a great disservice to those great strides in emancipatory virology, particularly those recapitulated in works such as Steve Goodman's analysis of the transformative contagiousness of dub in his *Sonic Warfare*, in conversation with the works of Kodwo Eshun and Paul Gilroy. My concern is distinctly Burroughsian to this extent; the writer's preoccupation, like my own, is with the virality of communication online amongst those of the New Flesh.

As was remarked earlier, the intrusion of cyberspace into the 'meat' is the only place where the writing, in the very text, the coding, precedes the digital territory and renders it as such, be it in the form of a textual 'post' or that of images and even video with audible components. Accordingly, the reality of what is discursively accepted becomes mediated through these controlled spaces—for example, the 'Q drops' of the augmented realities of 'Cosmic Right' cults like QAnon, various fact-checking or 'disinformation' series from mainstream outlets like the BBC, or even the established 'alternative' news sites themselves. For the New Flesh, events in meatspace derive their hyperreality from the digital categories, tropes, and memes that are found online, from which they receive their verification, their replicability, which is alike to the results of a scientific experiment. 'The real is produced from miniaturized cells, matrices, and memory banks, models of control—and it can be reproduced an indefinite number of times from these.'[40] They are 'hyper' real because when the real is verified by means of the online, the equivalence of the real to the online renders the latter as the site where the real is reproduced as something functionally identical with its digital rendering. It is therefore verified as more real than real. For example, 'lol' presents a laughter that does not require a relation to a previous act of laughing in meatspace for its meaning to hold. But hyperreality is not an impassible horizon, nor a nihilistic cause for despair, but a political and economic production that can be contested against. We can, and must, learn how to fight our media classes. Be it capitalist realism, Baudrillard, or Rupert Murdoch, there is an alternative.

The politics of hyperreality can be seen clearly in the moral panics inaugurated by our anglophone commentariat, where the report as written down and distributed becomes the gauge of the reality of its referent rather than the referent itself. The newspaper smear, the scaremongering against trans people being its most wretched recent manifestation, is treated as more real than the event. The word of genocidal forces is given precedent and verisimilitude by the ruling class, and they hold us to their words first, the map to the territory as they carve it upon us in blood. The press hold the public to account for what they themselves declare to be true of the public, for there is 'no smoke without fire', despite the fact that—as Abigail Thorn delightfully demonstrates with her recurring character in many *PhilosophyTube* videos—the press are often the real arsonists who set the public discourse ablaze with incendiary virality.

This used to be called 'lying', were it not the case that the function of the British commentariat is not to represent the real but increasingly to *produce it* in the realms of political representation, of marketing. To exist in British public life is to be measured by one's standing in regard to an ecosystem of hostile publications. If our Twitter-addicted, private-schooled media class register you as a threat, they will do their best as an immune system of empire to stochastically endanger you. They will delight in the fact that you cannot defend yourself by communications alone, given that the referent of their attack does not exist for you to apologize for or verify it. Their attacks have nothing to do with the 'truth' of representation, especially in the age of cyberspace communications. You cannot 'debate' or defeat them on a plane of representative reality, on communicative terms set by their strategic assault, for their communication is in so many senses pathological, a viral seeding of their codes to as many as possible who will carry them to both your destruction and the obstruction of alternative modes of life beyond this global death machine. *The Imperial press, liberal and conservative, are a mafia of bourgeois stochastic terrorists, drunk with spite and genocidal fervour, and they fucking hate you.* This requires a further exposition regarding the contemporary redundancy of 'representation', as has been so prominent in our previous cybernetic investigations.

The code under discussion does not represent anything—does not stand-in for the thing that it presents on the basis that it is to be treated *as if* the representation is equivalent to that which it represents—but rather enters a functional relationship, which attempts to produce what is coded as an expression of said code. This is where I would break with Richard Seymour's (albeit highly productive) definition of writing as 'marks on a surface intended to represent something for someone else'.[41] This is because it is not, first and foremost, a question of intention or representation, but the functional relations and processes of production that underly representation. And it is this infrastructure, in particular, that concerns both Seymour and myself—writing as production in the industry of contemporary cybernetic communication is the realm of the New Flesh.

For example, the posts on a website do not represent its coding, but rather express the code-content of the site as what we typically call 'content' as a transformation of the code, which does not change the body of the code or an 'incorporeal transformation' as Deleuze and Guattari would put it.[42] One does not change the code of YouTube by posting a video; one expresses its coding in the posted video, the posting of which is the event of such a transformation. To return to a previous example, for many users, those of the New Flesh, the word 'lol' no longer represents laughter. It no longer stands-in for the reality of a laugh 'in real life' (now 'irl'; this term has had a similar fate). Rather, it laughs for us—more real than real—and the term is increasingly used verbally within the 'irl' by those hooked into these media *instead* of laughter. In such instances, the verbal enunciation of this term now comes to represent that which previously mapped it out onto cyberspace, where it no longer needs to represent anything—its efficacy has gone viral and recoded the patterns of communication of those susceptible, those plugged into the addictive control circuits.

Before delving into the depths of viral word-communication, let us first return to the nature of the virus. Viruses infect bodies, modifying the processes within the infected to proliferate themselves by means of a further process of decoding and re-coding the codes which organize the infected organism. Viruses infect organized, organic units such as cells. Cells are enclosed unitary entities, singular functionaries that keep the macrocosm of tissues and organs composed of tissue structurally intact against contrary growths and tendencies of growth. *We* increasingly work according to scripts that treat our cognition, our experiential processes of thought and affect, as increasingly artificial and hypothetical. We are enclosed within assemblages of desks, we are connected to various objects that allow us to be productive, assembling us into phone-thumb-eye machines of writing and data-production. We are locked and enclosed into the cubicles of offices at home and away, which segment us into the cells of the spreadsheet. We are divided into cells: accounts, passwords, numerical values of credit score, the numbers that go into the landlord's bank account. We are digitized, that is, en-celled. Galloway perfects the definition of the digital as a real abstract process inaugurated by machines and the social relations that utilize them: '*The digital is the capacity to divide things and make distinctions between them. Thus, the digital appears to be quite explicitly a form of abstraction, if not simply abstraction as such.*'[43] We have been made digital, dividual, functional selves or *cellves*, and so we are primed for new viruses and viralities.

It is not to say that we were never susceptible to the following viralities before; rather, we have become, to a greater degree and extent, subjects defined by our potential as vectors for viral contagion. We increasingly melt into our digitized personae. We become addicted to our own PR campaigns, and hedge our posting in the public forum so that whatever is written attains either maximum relatability (categorical universality or fetishistic specificity, depending on the audience of potential infectees one wishes to cultivate) or an enduring and intoxicating notoriety. Either way, excitation through citation spreads the code, shares the love (especially when there's hatred involved). Citation is a perfect linguistic transmitter, surpassing even *real* viral entities, because one can cite into efficacy an image whose referent has never existed (the Necronomicon, the hidden masters, even the creed of the divine (*'Ein Gott, denn is gibt, gibt es nicht'* [A God that exists, does not exist]—Meister Eckhart)).

Whether viruses are alive or not is of no concern from the standpoint of cybernetic analysis, even as they manifest through animated matter. Viruses exist on what Mark Fisher called the 'flatline', they exist on the same plane as life does, interacting with life at the same time as the possibility of their un-alive nature suspends the rigidity of a distinction between the mechanistic and the vital. From a standpoint of cybernetic realism, it is not first and foremost what viruses *mean* in terms of the informational code they contain, but what viral processes and the transmission of that code *does* to the infected organism. When Deleuze and Guattari asserted that language is not at base communicational or informative—instead being primarily composed of commands and structures thereof, which order life through linguistic structures of habit and sense-making—they risked eliminating the political dimension of communication itself.

Such communication always engenders a command because, as Burroughs pointed out, 'communication is the action of propelling an impulse from a source point across a distance to a receiver point with the intention of bringing into being at the receipt point a duplication of that which emanated from the source point'.[44] I am commanding you, to the best of my ability, to think with the words I am typing here; and not only that, I am aiming to clarify what I say by explanation with this very sentence. I have a *sense*, that is to say, a contextual, informational, and intentional coding to these words. It is that sense that I am communicating on the level of both affect and the intelligibility of that which affects and is being affected by communication. In doing so, I attempt to use a linguistic force to produce a replication of this sense-code in your own mind. There is a communication established when there is a *degree* of replication achieved, although the sense of my words may not be as 'loud' to you. You may not get it to the fullest extent of my intention nor to the intensity of what I am writing, or you may even exceed the intensity of my intent in what we would call a hyperfixative or inspired mode of reading. Whilst I individualized the 'chain of command', so to speak, positing myself as its origin, I am not a self-caused being; it is the words that are really the command, and I am only carrying forth commands instilled in me. I am replicating—either intentionally, habitually, or unconsciously—*meanings* that I have been ordered to replicate until they become second nature, or within acceptable bounds of deviation. Linguistic or communicative inheritance, at least when it comes to institutional or dominant standards of grammar and of fixed domains of meaning, is always an inheritance of command. What we inherit here is also what we communicate back to ourselves: an active living history of chains of command, or to loosen the bonds a bit, chains of the ordering of sense and sensibility in making predicative judgements of the world.

This is the viral and replicative power of the terms of our order, and the word and image viruses that feed back into the integration of the New Flesh operate through this distinct logic of command. As Fisher points out, 'the basic form of digital communication is command: every time you pick up your smartphone, you've been told to do things. And even if they are friendly commands, nevertheless it's a massive stress on the nervous system.'[45] However, replication here must be severely qualified. No text will totally replicate itself in the receiver—nor could it, unless it contained all the codes of the reader's organism and somehow rewrote them totally into the codes of the text. Such an idea would be fine for an absurdist novel or screenplay, but it is far from what is being discussed here.

The process is instead one that we will describe as retroviral, meaning that viral code is inserted into the coding of the host, which then spreads the modified sequence (as opposed to being totally rewritten into a production factory for making virions, i.e., more virus-spreading microentities within itself). Retroviral processes are of course error-prone because, as the virologists put it, the mechanisms that convert (mediate) the code into a manner receivable to the host 'lack proofreading activity'.[46] In a much similar way, I can proofread my own text, but I cannot proofread *your experience of it*, never fully, and only provide negative feedback at best, guiding the reader as an additional process of communication. The code of this text will equally escape me (as much as theorists love to hedge their writings against possible misreadings and objections; this paranoiac mode of writing only presupposes the worst kind of readers, *other philosophers*). The author dies of a virus, but not a disease. The death of the author *is* virus and the virality that exceeds Him, and there is a surplus-value of code when it exceeds the initial communication where differential interpretation and further transmission becomes possible. From this mutation, the codes enter a new milieu through the receiver's new encoded function as a *provirus* carrying the edited sequence.[47] The virality of writing is the death of the author(ity), for there is no authority over the mutation of meaning. A classic example: the Gospels, biblical transmission of Christ. A modern example: Goethe's *The*

Sorrows of Young Werther goes viral. The Werther-virus inserts the codes of its titular character into the minds of Europe's proto-romantics, leading to a replication of his suicide in a wave of mass imitation (we're assuming Goethe didn't intend this, unless he made a Faustian bargain). What about post-modern examples of distributed texts mutating in terms of their meaning? Semiocapital has learned to capitalize on those; that's what the platforms are for. New ways to read everything, new ways to react to it. Surplus value functions as surplus meaning, surplus relevance, allowing for indefinite circulations and recirculations of the same memes for different circumstances.

It should be pointed out that there is no *a priori* necessity for any sense to be analytically contained within the words used, because words may be recoded, or they may take on associations as part of wider communicative assemblages, habits, and institutional practices of speaking. Slurs are reclaimed when the carrier is recoded for use in a certain environment where it flourishes as part of a new communal endearment. Cockney rhyming slang translates phonic resonance into codes, even to the point of redundancy. For example: Aris = Aristotle = bottle = bottle and glass = arse. The first term sounds practically the same as the resultant one, but only within a pragmatics established by the very process of Cockney semiosis and from within the proletarian milieu of its origin. Semiotic insurgency from below recodes and therefore risks infecting the terms of order, the ordering structures and codes of command, much like the viral zombie fantasy that recoils in horror at the hungry masses, which turn all solid social strata into wandering collectivities of meat.

There is, in some sense—pardon the pun—a mutual obligation imposed by the act of communication. You are called to respond and to replicate the sense-code, even to the point of suspending your disbelief in my use of these words for the sake of argument or curiosity. My codes are being imposed on your experiential and cognitive processes through a practice of literary composition. You aren't reading this in my internal monologue, because 'I' am not quite there behind the screen, unless I am reading it to you (and even then, that may be a recording, which is itself indifferent to whether I am currently alive or dead). It is instead the text itself that you are experiencing, which is making use of your interiority and sense organs. Nonetheless, this may not all be so distastefully 'one-sided', as the dialecticians would put it. There may be an obligation in the other direction, towards my own intent—ideally inseparable from that of the audience's takeaway from the book)—which I could be held to as my own *munus*, such as to an obligation to communicate powerfully (clearly, pleasurably, or in a gripping or addictive manner) to achieve adequate degrees of replication.

A writer writes with words in order to communicate. The writer communicates in order to rewrite something of the reader through degrees of code-replication (even when each party is the same person, but let's keep that feedback loop bracketed out for now), and absolutely wants the reader to spread the word about what is written. Public communicators especially always want virality of some degree. Martin Luther rewrote the German language *into* the language we know as the standardized *Hoch Deutsch* of today. 'Viral marketing' is its own field now, to the extent that it has become the everyday mode of self-capitalization, be it from corporations advertising products or individuals advertising a version of themselves written into social media *as a product*.

If the formal or functional activity is isomorphic, i.e., translatable, in terms of motions across an input-output relation of coding and re-coding/writing, then there is no need to speak of viruses metaphorically. The means of communication may be the carrier wave/viral capsid shell, or, as in the case of social media, the carrier wave and the code and processes of writing and encoding being carried may fade into an indifference to their differentiation. Burroughs once hypothesized about potential viruses of sound and light; if they could ever exist, it would be in a time like now. Advertisements, 'memes', emojis, franchises that exist to produce short image macros or GIFs of themselves rewrite our habits of speaking, thinking, and emoting. I am not making a value-judgement here. It may even be that semiotic or habitually affecting viralities are less parasitic than symbiotic, or they may even be beneficial to our capacities to experience the world and connect with each other. Maybe this is why it takes a properly systemic or cybernetic level of abstraction for us to see through the normativity that claims all virality to be hostility to the host, an invasion, rather than an opportunity to cultivate a viral hospitality towards new and exciting modes of becoming. (As the Derrideans love to point out, both hostility and hospitality share the same root, *hostis*). It is not that one should reiterate the Burroughsian cliché that 'language is a virus', but that the measure and success of communicative activity is proportion to its degree of viral replication or informational re-coding of the receiver.

Is the author, therefore, isomorphic with a virus? If we were to present a diagram of functionality, of inputs and outputs and communications of code between the author-text-reader assemblage and the virion-code-cell assemblage, we would see similarities in terms of writing and recoding in order to engineer a new functionality, yes. However, regardless of how pithy it would be to declare 'the author is a virus, and therefore I am a virus trying to rewrite you!', this would require us to adopt—even to be infected by—a bourgeois individualism about both authors and viruses. Viruses are not authors, nor are authors any sort of original or primary virions from whom viral processes ensue. There is no original act of intentional writing that the creator bequeaths to its environment from a separate, detached, creative interiority. As Barthes famously summarized, there is neither an authorial 'single "theological" meaning (the "message" of the Author-God) but a multi-dimensional space in which a variety of writings, none of them original, blend and clash'.[48]

I have just cited one now, and multiple before said citation. This text is being composed on a word processor, a screen of competing codes and writings, each of which have made some force on me as a producer of writing(s), and some which I may not even be consciously aware of. It would be no different if you were reading this on a computerized screen of some kind, and would possibly be even more effective as a presentation if there were competing texts from advertisements popping up, along with notifications from this or that social media site or email account: an agony (that is, an agonistic in the sense of competitive) array of codes and carriers competing for entry into the foci of your experience and mine, even as I write. The screen is a miraculous entity because it externalizes the barriers of sense, or at the very least redoubles it, such that codes and viral processes have more entry points and have an accelerated commute to any potential host.

So many codes have gone viral and their virality either lays dormant in me, has become the dominant coding that replicates itself (and therefore is less under consideration or detection by internal anti-viral immune systems, if not becoming the active code which immunizes itself against rewriting-infection), or is as yet undetected. The history of the codes of an organism in communication and community with itself and its environment is a history of competing forces of coding and decoding. The codes that organize an organism 'pool up' as its tendencies, swerves, and determinations (all with an aspect of mutability and chance). Some of these codes are benign, some malevolent to the continued organization of that organism as the life that it is, and some may be even beneficial in certain circumstances:

> Every cell in our body contains viral DNA. Human endogenous retroviruses, and elements thereof, make up about 8% of our genome. Most are inactive, fossil remnants from infections of germ cells that occurred over millions of years during our evolution. Some of them are suspected to be associated with specific diseases, but the regulatory sequences and protein products of other endogenous retroviruses have been coopted during our evolution for their unique functions. For example, retroviral gene products may play a role in the regulation of pluripotency in germ cells, in transmission of signals at neuronal synapses, and clearly in the way that we

> give birth. The development of the human placenta depends on cell fusion promoted by a retroviral protein. If not for these endogenous retroviruses, we might be producing our young in eggs, like birds and reptiles.
>
> Recent genomic studies have revealed that our viral "heritage" is not limited to retroviruses. Human and other vertebrate genomes harbor sequences derived from several other RNA and DNA viruses. As many of these insertions are estimated to have occurred some 40 million to 90 million years ago, this knowledge has provided unique insight into the ages and evolution of their currently circulating relatives. The conservation of some of these viral sequences in vertebrate genomes suggests that they may have been selected for beneficial properties over evolutionary time.[49]

All this to forfeit any sense of totally capturing any act of sense-production or encoding as 'original' or a-historical. Every creative act of writing or encoding therefore tends towards the creativity of sampling, of a chance consolidation of accumulated plunder surfing through flows of sense. These semioviral flows are increasingly *intense*, and even more so as we do not have to physically move our senseorgans to encounter them. To invoke a Deleuzoguattarian cliché, I, as a writer, am already quite a crowd in this text. I have already made myself several others more than the referent of 'I' through allegiances of citation, but there are also intrusions of communicative habits and the milieu of the writing process itself. It is not as if one writes a book from within a monastic cell, in one sitting, with no external communication and nothing that they would be replicating in the process of text-production. A hyperfixation with Burroughs here, the process of being surrounded by Deleuzoguattarians leaving me open to conceptual infection there, and catching a bout of COVID before viruses became a novel hyperfixation. Communication is inseparable from its environment, and a communicator is not as such without a community of established, habitual, and mandatory bounds of communicability. This may be what Hegel called *Ethical Substance*, or to put it more accurately and in materialist terms, this may be the relations of the production of sense and the conditions of recognized and recognizable sensibility, mediated by their histories of integration and difference into stratified functional relations.

Further, it should be noted that, etymologically, the *munus* of anything 'communal' or 'communicative' signifies an obligation in the form of a gift or debt to that which is connected in the common or communal situation. The opposite term for this is the *immune*. Someone immune to a virus is someone with whom it cannot communicate; an immunity from prosecution grants one (at least formally) a freedom from the obligation or public debt that is obedience to the law. This is not to say practically that the immune cannot become a vector for the ordering of what is communal—to say nothing of the immune as a state of exception or sovereign cardinal point around which a society can be ordered, such as a constitutional monarch—but that communication mediated through an immune body never penetrates into the body itself.

No immune cell has its code rewritten by such a viral event. Someone immune to a virus would instead be a vector only through transmission via, for example, viral matter on their hands, shoes, etc., of which they themselves share none of the risks of infection. It is therefore only a surface possibility of transmission. Whether one is immune or communal-communicative with the virus therefore only changes the mode of one's interaction with a virality. In the age of digital events of 'going viral' scaling in occurrence at the same time as bio-viral pandemics, viruses are already omnipresent.

Immunity, as a real function of exemption, is extrapolated to new extremes in the realm of capitalist economy, and especially as of late. Take the case of social democracy in Europe. A kind of localized social democracy in the imperial core nations and those close to them was itself a communal endeavour. It was the solicitation of an obligation to buy off some elements of the working and interstitial classes in order to keep the wider machine and its immune defences safe from an epidemic of communism, backed in part by a threat of nuclear force on the other side of Berlin (with immunological agents from the CIA and MI6 taking care of outbreaks in Chile and the rest of Latin America).

With the defeat of Soviet and Democratic communism, what Bataille once called the last '*obligation*' of wealth has fallen, and with it the *munus*.[50] The mandatory contributions of Christian charity and poor relief as established by the authority of the Divine Author of the World have fallen to the voluntaristic authority of the *owners* of the world. Ownership means nothing other than to enclose and protect what is being enclosed, to erect great immune systems against others. They now believe themselves to have total immunity from the communist virus the world over, and stratify new forms of immunity in the same manner.

The hegemonic powers of the Earth have only feared a few viruses; among them sit the Black Death, Ebola, SARS-CoV-2, and Communism. Yet they had little fear of their own virality, the virality of capital, and had no issue condemning whole civilizations to viral genocide with their transmission of pathogens across the sea in colonization. As Sonali Gupta and H. Bolin point out, viral deaths are acceptable so long as they do not disrupt vital nodes in the transmission and flow of capital. This is why, unlike COVID, international mitigation efforts 'have not been seen for viruses such as dengue or yellow fever, even though they still cause mass deaths in Latin America, Southeast Asia, and Africa'.[51]

With the defeat of communization comes immunification, and this fits well the state of affairs that Donatella de Cesare calls 'Immunodemocracy', the purest distillation of negative liberty: '*noli me tangere*. This is all that the citizen requires of democracy: do not touch me.'[52] Now, of course, this was always part of the deal within the nominally 'democratic' capitalist nations: a qualified immunity from *seeing* the products of their society on the basis that they give a little for their upkeep, which culminated in the great welfare states of the mid-20th century. Such profitable charity predates these systems; nonetheless, even Friedrich Engels saw their prevailing tendency. Here I could not help myself but be compelled by the force of its encoded sense to communicate to you a passage from *The Condition of the Working Class in England*:

> let us hear the English bourgeoisie's own words. It is not yet a year since I read in the *Manchester Guardian* the following letter to the editor, which was published without comment as a perfectly natural, reasonable thing:
>
> > "MR. EDITOR,– For some time past our main streets are haunted by swarms of beggars, who try to awaken the pity of the passers-by in a most shameless and annoying manner, by exposing their tattered clothing, sickly aspect, and disgusting wounds and deformities. I should think that when one not only pays the poor-rate, but also contributes largely to the charitable institutions, one had done enough to earn a right to be spared such disagreeable and impertinent molestations. And why else do we pay such high rates for the maintenance of the municipal police, if they do not even protect us so far as to make it possible to go to or out of town in peace? I hope the publication of these lines in your widely circulated paper may induce the authorities to remove this nuisance; and I remain,– Your obedient servant, "*A Lady*."
>
> There you have it! The English bourgeoisie is charitable out of self-interest; it gives nothing outright, but regards its gifts as a business matter, makes a bargain with the poor, saying: "If I spend this much upon benevolent institutions, I thereby purchase the right not to be troubled any further, and you are bound thereby to stay in your dusky holes and not to irritate my tender nerves by exposing your misery. You shall despair as before, but you shall despair unseen, this I require, this I purchase with my subscription of twenty pounds for the infirmary!" It is infamous, this charity of a Christian bourgeois![53]

Engels—doing his best Max Stirner impression there (oh, what might have been!)—illustrating how the *munus* used to operate. The ruling class of the imagined community of the nation, itself a community that grants the economy of said nation a defining and governing tendency for replicating itself, immunizes its own viral propagation from seizure or destruction by the communist virus and from codes that disgust or disrupt it by means of 'charity', itself coded as a social 'health' (*for whose socius?*). In the ruins of welfarism, only the bourgeois Lady's last invocation stands guard to protect her and her ilk—*the municipal police*. Luckily for her lot, policing has gone viral, and any citizen may reveal themselves a cop,[54] or deputize themselves, depending on degrees of immunity or proximity to immune systems.

Immunization can itself go viral insofar as you can be encoded in order to replicate the community as it is dominantly structured—the contest concerning virality is a civil war over social reproduction. This is because we are all contested productive entities and viral spaces. We are potential hosts for the capitalist viruses, be they libidinal, affective, etc. But we are also immanently plastic potential hosts for something else—everyone is at least a *potential* viral insurgent without the right passcodes and immunificatory clearances.

Dominant community-virality makes sure we are always able to check up on each other, either by making ubiquitous the ability to turn each other into *content* (from which social capital may be extracted through a panopticism of the phone and camera), or by writing the heroic ego into the self-deputizing weaponized 'operator', who places the source of a homeless cry of despair in a fatal chokehold. This latter function is the viral image of the 'good man with a gun', the proliferating fantasy of the 'shoot first, ask questions later' cop. The authority of the authors of satirical comics like 2000AD's *Judge Dredd* and Marvel's *The Punisher* was undermined by the fact that the Thatcherite and Reaganite dismantling of the welfare state was a far more favourable environment to the virus of policing, its recoding and deterritorializing of the images of state violence, and the investment of large swathes of the public's desire towards them. Where this could not work, surveillance went viral in the case of the recoding of home-based wire taps (such as Amazon's Alexa) as conveniences, and constant video recording as 'content production', which thrives on viral desires of viral fame. Yet the death of the author in this equation means that no such 'self' goes viral; rather, virality is assigned to the codes that the self can carry within its environment. The 'author' of a viral event is a precondition, a launch site; what goes viral is the code-content in which one might gain a return-investment with the right encoded signature (like and subscribe!).

In light of a sense of the virality and biopolitics of our class landscape, it could be possible to determine one's proximity to the imperial core (or nodes thereof) by means of charting zones and processes that the immune pass through ceaselessly without being subject to their own systems, be it by access to healthcare and vaccinations or by the manner in which they smoothly pass through the immune systems we call 'borders'. These borders, these immunational systems, are the membranes that have themselves allowed the rich (and their subsidiary functionaries in fractions of the petit bourgeoisie) to become perfect vectors for viral contagions, such as COVID, of which they had only qualified immunity due to their class-based access to medical resources. Yet, before attempting to map the viral efficacy of dominant codes and coded machineries of social production and social reproduction, one must first consider what it means to think of virality in terms of domination as such. At the same time, we must also grasp the limits of virality for such ends in light of the possibility of mutation, of a virality that can subtract or overwrite codes of authority.

Major and Minor Virality: Reproduction and Replication

> Our virus infects the human and creates our image in him.
>
> William S. Burroughs, *Nova Express*[55]

The distinction between major and minor virality is not a simple matter of quantification. A major virality is not 'major' by virtue of the number of infected. Major and minor do not function to distinguish between pandemics and local outbreaks according to a numerical threshold of cases. When I describe something as major, I also do not mean that it is a majority by virtue of having a higher relative quantity than that which is minor or 'the minority'. Instead—and here I am drawing wholeheartedly on Deleuze and Guattari—what is major or minor is a matter of function, organization, and therefore necessarily political power and its distribution also.

Deleuze and Guattari prefer to invoke language and dialect as their main examples for this distinction and it is worth joining them in this. When the ruling forces of England after 1066 spoke French, French was the major language in England, despite the relative scarcity of speakers of French against the vast quantity of the population who spoke with Old English, Cornish, Welsh, etc., as 'minor' languages, for these tongues did not give a defining identity for the political *status quo*. Rather, their minority (and therefore the majority) was produced as a function of their feudal domination.

Famously, we can see this division built into Modern English—that is, 'modern' in the sense that the English spoken today exists after English became a major language, having murderously suppressed its Celtic neighbours' tongues, in making itself a majority in Eire, Kernow, Cymru, etc. The distinctions built into Modern English are materially produced on the level of class stratifications—for example, between the etymologies of those words that refer to the livestock one worked with versus the eventual meat-product that was consumed (and rarely by the peasantry). The cow (sharing roots from the Germanic *Kuh*) is worked on; the beef (from the French *bœuf*) is consumed. One can name additional examples, such as the prejudice against African American Vernacular English, or the very existence of 'High German' or 'received pronunciation' as 'the Queen's English'. The majority-function is a function of the production and reproduction of a status, against which other tendencies, potentials, or becomings are rendered as minor.

The proletariat are not the major term of the world system, despite their quantitative outnumbering of their oppressors who set the terms of order, who erect themselves as the major, the dominant and dominating part of the capitalist system. The bourgeoisie in this binary are the overcoding term: that part which unifies, i.e. captures, the proletariat within the function of selling their labour where they have nothing else; and this part enacts this function by ongoing processes of dispossession and accumulation enacted upon the quantitatively gargantuan masses of humanity (and all other life on this planet). A majority does not become a minority by being outnumbered, but only through the deposing and de-activation of the political machineries by which it is able to produce itself as the dominant coding of the material world—that is, of the territory in which it determines the *status quo* and the corresponding subjectivity of that code. The major is the dominant and dominating function or set of functions of a social-political system, material on the objective level of institutions, distributions of resources, etc., and subjective in that it structures predominant modes of language, communicative sense, and consciousness according to schemas of subjectivity, which are expressions of these dominant social codes.

Having introduced the notion of the major here, I argue that a major virality—understood as a function in terms of the operations it carries out—is a virus of domination: of the production of authority of its code and of the *reproduction* of this authority-code. The most explicit viral image of this would be the image of the virus that reduces an organism into a thing that exists simply for the sake of reproducing this virus by producing more virions, but a retroviral image would also be adequate insofar as we explain these viral and retroviral movements according to the same function. Namely, in the case of a major virality, both images would depict the rewriting of the organism in terms of the violent imposition of a limit to the being it is attached to. The first virus reduces the creative and operational potential of the cell to the production of virions, exhausting it unto death. The latter (major) retrovirus would be the transcription of a code into the receiving body, which overwrites, restricts, or deletes existing codes in such a manner that the range of activities and functions said body can enact becomes limited by the additional code—it adds in order to subtract. Codes are replicated for the sake of a reproduction of the major, and the reproduction of the society coded by the same major tendencies. Majority is a product, not its original producer, and yet it nonetheless plays a part in its own reproduction through a menagerie of machineries at its disposal—like those of the factories, amongst which are the machineries of major virality.

Viral social reproduction needs its viruses, its codes, to distribute. As the great tradition of socialist-feminist social reproduction theory has demonstrated, the prime examples lie in the cases of the family as the unit of social reproduction and of the codification of gender roles established in terms of a gendered division of labour as well as the policing of both before a major standard (that is, heteronormative and cisnormative). *Calm*. I am not calling anyone's mother or father, daughter or son, nan, grandad, second cousin, etc., a disease. I will not call for any sense of 'cure', nor would I care to communicate in such a register. Virality is not in and of itself malicious or 'bad', nor does every virality produce pathogenesis (which is a question of utility and ultimately one of value). Think less of any loved ones and more about the politics of *family values* that gets shored up in the face of social crises. The major family-virus is a virus of *archetype*, breaking that word down into its components of *arche* as principle or command and the *type* as category. The category exists for the sake of judgement; of identifying X under the category Y, which stabilizes this identification. All categories are bordered, universal, for all X, such that X is in category Y and thus holds the predicate denoted by said category. Unmarried men are bachelors confined by the rigidity of the definition, but it is not as if this boundary has required much reinforcement. However, those confined within the coding of a category—such as a major standard of masculinity, femininity, binary gender or sexual dimorphisms, racial categories,

categories of the 'normal', etc.—are actively confined insofar as the borders are socially, politically, and economically—that is to say, materially—stratified. It is not that such structures are always necessarily *experienced* as confinement; regardless, there is a real material consequence to stepping outside of them, be it a loss of material support in the act of departure (not qualifying for any or inadequate welfare, healthcare, the support of other family members etc.), or with the additional active persecution of those who blur or transgress the category (including those categorized as abnormal for the sake of that very persecution).[56]

The communication of the standard—that is, the inherently political majority—familial unit has gone viral, or rather, has been virally active for centuries as distributed through patriarchal legal codes, colonial-cultural violence, and religious-conservative orthodoxies. A system communicates this standard to adults in the hope that they will produce children, who will be communicated the values of family in a dual motion of social and parental transmission. This process is itself made of gendering, sexuating viruses, which code the body into a given 'biological' functionality and social role. One's sex and gender are *assigned*, written of someone as judgement, as *categorical* statement, as a 'stable' identification (and indeed, often inscribed upon their bodies surgically in the assignment of intersex infants). That the Fascisti of today mobilize themselves around transphobia is also partially a terror of the rewriting of the already minor potentialities of language, which exceed the major and lay dormant within its composition. This can be seen in the political mobilization against 'pronouns', or the active effort to prevent people from changing their gender or sex markers on official documents (which ultimately have no immediate necessity to be recording such categories at all), such as driving licences, passports, banking, etc. It is not that the transphobes are protective of grammar as such, that they are linguistic prescriptivists, but that they fear the disruption of the safe confinement of the codes that stabilize the territory of social experience (including their own). Society constantly communicates one's gender, one's sex, and even one's family to one's self through the address, the name, the assumed pronoun, etc., and intensify the process of rewriting one's coding through the insertion of such limiting codes constantly (blue for boys, pink for girls; boys play X, girls play Y). The categories become second nature, habit, part of the *community* of communication to which sense is limited in terms of these codes (or rather, which these codes attempt to limit).

To speak of processes of virality is not to automatically commit oneself to pathologization, reducing the output of a viral process to disease. The paradigm of the understanding of virality here is that of informatics, and there is no need to retreat back to Koch and work backwards from the disease to the effectuating viral matter. This is not a discourse of health, but a discourse of code, inscription, and hegemony via the functional relationships of communication and the viral process. To be content and flourishing within one's own gender or sex assignment from birth is not, therefore, being described as a *disease* any more than having a happy relationship with one's parents is, or indeed being a parent. It is not the case that people have been totally captured and turned into viral automata—for all viral communication is a matter of degree anyway, as articulated above—nor is it the case that they have been necessarily 'duped' into total identification with any function assigned to them. Even at a higher degree of comfort, integration, resonance, or adequation to a major code, the major code remains as an abstraction, a universal, and every body is particular. *People are not piloted by the codes retrovirally communicated to them; rather, they are supplemented by them.* No one simply serves to produce and reproduce the universal in their lives, for neither we nor our actions are reducible to code any more than we are reducible to genetic codes and to our mere capacities for action as individuals. Each individual also enjoys and expends the particularity, the life-time, of their own finite existence, and we will never achieve any infinite equivalence or permanent reduction of ourselves to a concept, or even to language itself. People always hold their unnameable, unique ownness, which resists their total disappearance into universals such as 'The People'.

The surplus-value of code—the explosive plasticity, the possibility of mutation—always maintains an active resistance against total subsumption to varying degrees, and the plasticity that our bodily capture and inscription presupposes is never exhausted entirely, insofar as the capture and reproduction thereof actively presupposes it. Major viruses are not impervious to mutation by which minorities can, and often do, indeed flow out of them (to return to the examples of the majority of English and the minorities of slang). To live as a man is not to be the category 'man', and the virality of man-as-a-virus is not the same as any one man, but is instead the process by which man as the major, dominating function of a binary system is produced and reproduced in a heteropatriarchal society. Therefore, whilst I disagree with Xandra Metcalfe when she claims that cissexuality is the 'true social pathogen', it is predominantly on the level of the technicality that detaches virality from pathology.[57]

There is no need to pathologize (or even pathologically moralize) now that virality can be understood in terms of an informatics of code and a dynamic of communicative forces. The task, however, is to *politicize* the distribution of codes and the imposition of limits by major viral processes. The major virus encodes in order to limit that which it rewrites, inscribing a delimited function that operates by proliferating said code in a process of viral replication, itself serving the ends of reproducing the stability of a social system. Major viruses add code for the sake of bounding the potential of a body by organizing it around an additional function of replicating and transmitting that code.

Contrastingly, what I term a minor virality similarly adds or rewrites code in order to subtract from an order that constitutes it as a subjected or subjugated pole of a social binary: that introduces an element of subtraction from the majority, which renders it minor. Where the major virus adds code for the sake of bounding potentiality in the form of a limit, a minor virality adds or rewrites code such that limit-codes are weakened, deactivated, or rendered mutable. There is a preciously continental philosophical pun to be made here to summarize the difference. Major viralitics infect in supplementing a *delimitation* of possibility, whereas minor virality is the *de-limiting* of that which opens up possibilities through the insertion of a de-limiting code, which may even accelerate code-mutation by removing obstacles to communication with other minor, oppressed codes. Minor virality subtracts the unifying, limited element that domination encodes. A virus is minor as that which produces lysis, rupture, of the limits encoded by the major forces. Fanon declares at the beginning of his decolonial project of psychoanalytic subtraction that he seeks 'a complete lysis of this morbid body'.[58]

The first recorded minor virus was written down in order to defuse it by rendering it comedic: *Virus Lysistrata*—the virus communicated through the minority of women within all the realms of Greece, so that the military capacities of the major stratum of Man would grind to a halt while those women who accepted the code of Lysistrata occupied the Acropolis. Lysistrata names the virus of solidarity and tactical excellence that comprehends the unity of economies of desire and of finance, of social reproduction and the cybernetics of patriarchy. In occupying the Athenian treasury at the same time as they began an indefinite sex strike, the women of all warring lands succeeded in severing the flows of libidinal and financial investment at the same time as withholding the labour of social-sexual reproduction. It took a dialectician's intervention, brought in by Aristophanes, in the form of the Goddess of 'Reconciliation', who halts the narrative of resistance, such that everyone goes back to their original roles. Yet there can be no such reconciliation with the Major today, none with the forces that govern our world: extermination or communism is the choice.[59]

The enemies, the fascists, the phobes, do not understand minor virality very well (and yet enough to be terrified by it); instead, they render their objects-to-be-destroyed in major viral terms, as a minority competing for the major position of the dominant end of a constructed binary system. For example, the recurring reactionary fear that gay or trans people are 'reproducing' themselves via 'social contagion'—that is, by their very public existence as well as working in schools, etc.—is an admission of the major virality of their own mode of cisheteronormative-familial (apologies to whoever is doing the audiobook, even if it's myself) social reproduction. Their fearful analysis is grounded on the admission of virality as well as a capitalistic framing of competition, as if there were competing brands in a child-producing industry. Indeed, this is what heteropatriarchy has so often constructed and reduced people with wombs to: matrimonially appropriated means of production.

The assault on queer community is an assault on the inherent queerness of communication, the death of authority before the inevitability and the inherency of difference, which exceeds any univocal 'essence', presenting itself as simultaneously genetic (in the sense of both genes and of being innately tied to the origin of the organism) and immutable. The enemy looks at a can of beer endorsed by a trans celebrity and, supplemented by the major virus of cisgender supremacy, enters a state of immunological shock. This is because, for them, any degree of the communication of queer codes is itself enough to risk the spread of a minor virus, which detaches those whom it encounters from the limits imposed by, for example, mandatory, permanent gender assignments. Before cisheteronormative and familial modes of social reproduction, any other code becomes pathogenetic. It becomes the source of a social 'disease' insofar as it is seen as a threat to the dominant codes, according to which the flow of future humans are to be produced in the reproduction of society—of the future *workers* and fresh functionaries of capital, especially the *human capital*, which we all are under neoliberalism. It is human capital that intensifies its regime in the contemporary data economy, where everything can become capital as *content*, and therefore can be produced as data for a personal brand that feeds back upon us in the addictive production of New Flesh.

What is major or hegemonic in societal ordering can issue viral transmissions from itself in the form of an immune response. The use of viruses against viruses has been one of the most viral revolutions in medicine: cowpox against smallpox, etc., 'chickenpox parties' of exposure and the like, and even the COVID boosters that have saved so many from that choking hell. I am not talking about vaccines but major viruses of word and image, which supplement social communications with additional senses and imaginaries that mark minorities out for targeting, isolation and/or active destruction, encoding them with markers hostile to their ability to communicate, to be in community, with others. Antisemitism, for example, is just such a virus, where the antisemite attacks the image circulated of the Jewish person. The racist caricature is the additional coding, the viral supplement built into the communicative fabric of an antisemitic culture or intensified through the circulation of viral communications, which infect experiences of the world with codes of pre-judgement.[60]

We can see today where the channelling and coding of semioviral flows of sense and media service function as a device of stochastic terrorism. One need only look to the ways in which expressions of solidarity with Palestinians against genocide by the Israeli state have been the object of an attempt by Western media outlets to overcode them with the supplement that renders them as 'terrorists' identical with Hamas. With this viral supplement pumped out through columns and legacy media, the aim is to delegitimize resistance at the same time as it legitimizes them as a target for attack (as the label 'terrorist' so typically functions). Semioviral flows coded by hegemonic forces are an immunological response to a resistance that refuses the meaning given by the consensus of the day.

When systems come under pressure in the reproduction of society, and in response to minor communication (which in public life is even the merest *visibility* to society), hegemonic communications systems—such as the right-wing, liberal, and even elements of the 'leftist' press, bitter about their own political irrelevance—issue their own word-viral transmissions in the form of gay and trans panics (not that the two are in any way separable from the perspective of minority). One of the most egregious examples of this was the encoding of an *actual virus*, HIV, as a 'gay plague', invoking a sense of punishment for 'immorality', and the attempt to spread virally the encoding that queer identity is a matter of reproduction not *of* the child, but *through* the child in the ongoing panics over 'exposure' to such codes. The most famous immunofascistic practices, however, have always been genocidal, be it in the rewriting of the souls of millions via the major viral processes built into colonial schooling (for example, the residential schools in Canada, but essentially any colonial education system), or the burning of the Institute for Sexual Science in Germany in the 1930s and its library, from which we do not yet know if queer knowledges in Europe have recovered.

In the latter case, it is important to highlight that the fascists did not burn books because they were *books*—i.e., because they hated the idea of communicative knowledge that the idea of a book *represents*—but rather because of what *these books* could do by virtue of what is coded in their pages. There is a liberal, Orwellian idea, touted by ideologues of the current 'free' press, that books and literature—the mere presence of ideas and difference among them as manifest in a given plurality of books—inherently stand for some kind of free exchange of information and ideas simply by virtue of being books. However, as private items and commodities alone, they cannot stand for anything other than an exchange value. A bookshop can stand for this to a degree: yes, a book *promoting* such ideas can stand for those ideas in turn, but it acquires that supplemental coding from its production and its social relations in order to do so. For a book to stand for access to knowledge and open flows of information beyond this value, it requires social relations of social ownership—a commonly owned library, perhaps. But even then, the book no longer needs to 'represent' anything, for its existence is a function of those very relations, which make those ideas actualities, actual powers manifest in material configurations of our lives as a reading public.

So, the enemy did not burn Hirschfeld's library because of their hatred for learning generally, but as an immunological measure. Every book was a virion, a means of supplementing the code of the reader in such a manner that their possibilities of becoming expanded beyond the code-confines of the present, or even allowed them to better understand the codes, feelings, interpretations of their own bodies and consciousness, which they had already been living with beyond the codes of the norm.

Yet even this analysis is deficient, as the genocidal violence of the destruction of the Institute for Sexual Science was not simply an attack on books, but on all media of communication, which bore such codes—notably, the vast collection of photographs of homosexual, transgender, and intersex subjects as a documentation of the LGBTQI subculture of Germany at the time. All of these were communicators that, in their own way, answered Spinoza's question of 'what can a body do?', and they answered beyond the imposed limits that the major viralities had failed to write out of them. For this, they were targeted as a social disease, antagonistic to the production of 'pure', 'healthy' society, and thus marked for destruction. Photographic panels, which held such photos for the sake of educating wider audiences beyond the specialized tomes of scientific research written by Hirschfeld et al., were equally the targets of the Nazi raiding parties.[61] That vast amounts of questionnaires—which bore the personal recordings of the lives of so many trans, intersex, and gay subjects—survived, as Heike Bauer notes, was due to the impracticality of disassembling that section of the archive. The enemy believed their spectacle of semiotic destruction to be enough.[62]

The enemy has failed to eliminate the codes that terrified them in Germany in the 1930s, and they will not cease to fail. The data-production lines that have made possible the New Flesh have also allowed for an active and minor mutation of the archive as such. A major archive is the presence and recording of stratified and sanctioned data, arranged and edited according to categories that form inputs as they are catalogues and stored within. A minor archive—which we may playfully call an *an-archive*—gathers and presents *transformations*, productions and demonstrations of mutability, rather than a catalogue of the immutable. I do not speak of this concept as an author thereof, but as a transmitter and a receiver of the notion of a 'viral' or 'everywhere' archive from Mel Y. Chen's work on gender transition in the age of cyberspace and of YouTube. Chen highlights examples of archives made by Asian transgender men, which demonstrate the (an-)archival potentials of transition rendered online, for the ways each

> presume, in their own ways, that identities are not preset. They are live, constructed, presentist, futurist, real. In their dynamism, their virtuality, their interconnectedness, their evanescence, their craft, and their readiness, these archives might be thought of as viral: not alive, since digital; not dead, since mobile. They are not archived reliably, and so they must be concocted again and again; even if identity itself is forestalled and forestalled and forestalled, the archives make and make.[63]

These *an*-archives transmit transformation without delimiting it in advance. It is this transmission, this virality, of subtraction for the sake of transformation, which allows for the promise of transformative self-determination. This promise is not made with any certainty of escape from that which would prevent its fulfilment, yet it presents us with a relative degree of what is possible under the Corporate Platform Complex that constitutes cyberspace under capitalism—of a transformation of the New Flesh. This is not the promise of cyberspace as it was first iterated—that is, as it was sold to us. There is no freshly discovered digital continent upon which we may find our new, true selves. There is only transmission and mutation, against the confinement of control.

Major virality aims to produce us as information and immunize the social body against deformity, in the sense of the rupture of the forms of social production and reproduction. It is a concept that highlights a set of tools, orientations, or tendencies that embrace deformation as transformation. Resistance, not reconciliation. The task of the New Flesh is to refuse Aristophanes' immunological defacement of the Lysistrata virus, instead virally arresting the flows of capital, to expand the an-archive and to maximize the transmissibility of its transformations through the communization of cyberspace. The communization of cyberspace is not the communization of another world, but a part of our world. To communize cyberspace is to begin a process of abolition against the social relations that render it what it is today: those of capitalist production. What is online is not a new territory, but an intensive mapping, a product of the world. It is not a space of the possible, but something very much actual in its structure—that is, the real material infrastructure of the economies of data and the new circuitries of imperialism. If it cannot be communized, then let it collapse under the weight of its own transformations, let loose upon the digital world, across the semioviral flows of resistance. The question whether the New Flesh can be emancipated, or whether we should be emancipated *from* the circuits that render us as New Flesh, is a matter of politics before it is a matter of mere technology. For now, in the melee of meaning that manifests in our discursive and strategic contestations, both online and offline, let a thousand minor viralities bloom.

POSTSCRIPT: THE LABOUR OF ARTIFICIAL INTELLIGENCE AND THE DIGITAL PLANTATION

Nothing would be more neglectful than to conclude this investigation of the New Flesh without confronting the latest developments in the data economy as they stand in relation to the global political situation, as well as in relation to themselves. In contrasting their dominant images to their actual conditions of appearing, the latest luminaries of techno-capital always show themselves as mere posting, vaporware. Data streams, as commodity flows, can nourish many a capitalist beast. The latest chimera is 'AI'—those generative playthings that provoke fear whilst soliciting us to further stimulation, as one fumbles with the latest digital toy. It is with these machines that we can return the production and mediation of data to its margins, to the peripheries of the global economy, in which data is not simply the secretion of a simultaneously stimulated and stupefied populace in the global North.

As we started, so we shall end: the politics of the machine precedes its actualization, for what is actual must come to be before it ultimately is. Let me dispense with any charity in interpreting the meaning of these new machines, because their meaning is not conceptual; the concept of 'AI' refers to nothing real about the machines we encounter when we engage with any system given such a label. I flat out refuse to entertain any fantasy of 'Artificial Intelligence' on the level of its superficial possibility when discussing any actual machines that are described as such.

'AI' nonetheless already has a kind of agency due to its hype. The intensity of our manufactured excitement and anxiety in the anticipation of its presence remains a site of libidinal and financial investment. It is a marketable and marketing image, and in the age of its marketing, we cannot speak about it publicly as if we were talking about a merely analytic, abstracted thought experiment. I will not consider AI as a speculative possibility of constructing cognition in a non-human agent, but first and foremost as a political image that has a corresponding economic and political actuality, which precedes and *must* precede a merely philosophical interpretation of it. I am not interested in the philosophy of minds that *could* be; I am enraged at the minds and bodies that are enslaved to the maintenance of the economy by which our comfortable deliberations become possible.

In brief, the thesis is that the autonomy of 'Artificial Intelligence'—that is, the 'self' part of its supposed self-organization, which is often touted as becoming autonomous even from humanity itself—is a bourgeois mystification. It is a hype machine, a marketing machine, and through it we can illuminate the labour relations of the data-economy and the intensifying tendencies of what Deleuze and Guattari called 'machinic enslavement'. Such enslavement is not merely opposed to a machinic production of subjectivity, but may indeed be the reduction of human lives to components in a machine, within which a controlled subjectivity is one of many outputs. The unifying principle of this machine and its production is its servility to capital and its empire.[64]

If we were to truly gaze upon these machines, these platforms, these 'AIs', as well as the sources of their data sets and moderation, as the computational prisons of labour that they are, we would be justified in shuddering before their falsity. We would shudder in recognizing that we too are confined and en-celled within their cybernated zones of control, and that our autonomy is no less of a lie in their presence.[65] If no such cybernation can be saved, de-activated, redeemed, or communized, so be it. What I have aimed to do in this book is to provide new conceptualizations adequate to our times and to my experience of them, and I will continue to do so with an immanent critique of 'Artificial Intelligence' and its real presuppositions. AI is nothing artificial, but a multifarious malevolence of data as an intensifying source of dead labour.

Let us start with the abstraction capital has given us: this notion of 'Artificial Intelligence', which has thankfully been pre-mediated by one of cybercapital's most totalizing monoliths. It is true that the capitalist class have succeeded in creating AI of a sort, but this is not ChatGPT or DALL·E; it is a network of systems that produce the effects of intelligence, by centralizing and capturing through employment cognitive work—what Jeff Bezos once called 'artificial artificial intelligence' or 'AAI'.[66] Taking this as a simple double negation, we are left with 'I', the 'I' or self of an AI, which is anything but artificial.

This 'I' is that of the worker inserted within relations of employment, centred around data production and the regulation of data processing via corrective feedback inputs on the outputs of digital systems. Bezos' 'AAI' refers to the workers of the Amazon Platform Mechanical Turk—itself named after a machine designed to play chess whilst giving the appearance of machinic intelligence and autonomous operation, but which contained a hidden human operator. The platform assigns human workers tasks that originally centred around correcting undesirable algorithmic outcomes around Amazon listings, such as the algorithm's inability to recognize duplicate products. Workers who sign up for such platforms, including others such as Clickworker and Appen, are all assigned tasks on a precarious basis, in the sense that they're paid per task—a gig rather than a standard waged position.

I worked for Appen for a number of years for extra cash, that and Lionbridge AI, where various tasks (usually only doable once a day) involved checking the accuracy of automated translations, or rating advertisements on Instagram and Facebook based on desirability and legibility. A further task involved validating whether search queries returned accurate results. My job, like that of any other microworker, was functionally to provide feedback to these machineries. The cognition of the microworker is the motor that, when plugged into the microwork platform, produces data-feedback and feedback-data for the refinement of algorithmic processes. As this stuff is less appetizing or fun than the infinite scroll, what little cash there is exists as an incentive. But this is a multi-billion-dollar industry, with millions of workers worldwide. In 2021, a conservative estimate put the value of the AI market as reaching $122 billion by 2022.[67] The average wage of the precariat enclosed within Amazon's Mechanical Turk is $2 an hour, with an individual task paying sometimes as little as 20 American cents.[68]

The work of corrective feedback manifests further in content moderation, filtering out harmful (or more accurately, *copyrighted*) material on social media platforms, as well as 'AI' platforms like ChatGPT. ChatGPT is, of course, not a cognition machine, but a human-moderated, human-constructed, and indeed human-powered machine, which takes texts produced by humans and then recombines them in tandem with *human* feedback in order to produce textual outputs that resemble patterns of writing in reference to certain functions of communication, i.e., topics and explanations. It is at best a machine that cultivates the habits we have and mimics them, and it can do so precisely because it is *not* conscious, and therefore not self-conscious, and therefore not self-editing other than as a habit granted to it by human moderation. Left to its own devices, it does nothing; yes, but equally, left to its own products, it passes into nonsense.

ChatGPT's data set may still require constant moderation as to its outputs, but that data set is cut off at 2021. You don't feed cows other cows; you don't feed a machine that eats human input its own excretions and cybernetic-kin (a disgusting anthropomorphization from me there). This has nothing to do with any kind of Turing-Cop situation—there is no intervention here from what Land would call a 'Human Security System', which is trying to prevent the birth of a planetary intelligence that supersedes the confines of bourgeois humane subjectivity and its conditions of experience. Rather, such an 'AI' would be given the machinic, semiological equivalent of a prion disease, Bovine Cyberform Encephalopathy.

It is telling as to how much pathologization is linked to productivity and capacity rather than experience or consciousness that our 'Artificial Intelligence' luminaries have managed to bring machinic sickness so close to actuality *before* they succeeded in their greatest fears of producing cybernetic consciousness. This is to be expected because, as David Bentley Hart once explained to my colleagues and me in some detail in an episode of *Acid Horizon*, *we are not software*. Humanity is the ground of these technologies, the dark ground of the territory beyond the mapping, which reduces us to the abstraction of data and the object of capitalist strategy. As Schelling used to say, 'anarchy lies in the ground'.[69] These machines need human flesh, old and new, upon which these edifices of feedback are erected.

In its need for human mediation, it seems the 'artificially intelligent' machine *itself* should be addicted to feedback (if it could be worthy of such a state at all). Yet our grammatical structures of language betray an ontological leap that is simply false. 'The machine' may be able to occupy the subject position of a sentence and be attributed a predicate, but the machine is not subject to itself—its self-consciousness lies outside itself in the workers and managers that collectively produce it. Such machines may provide outputs that resemble those produced by cognition without the element of subjectivity, but purposiveness, the appearance of purpose, and agency are by no means the same thing. In this sense, the uncriticality of this use of the term 'intelligence' is truly fascinating. Intelligence is here invoked as the ultimate 'seems like' image, a mere *vibe*, based on the assumption of a quantifiability, a fixity or essence to intelligence, which cannot but tend in the most eugenic directions as opposed to any kind of ethical relation with otherness. Under such a view, it takes intelligence as a *resource*, one isomorphic with human capital.

If such things were intelligent, then the charlatans at OpenAI—or whatever company is currently begging parliaments across the globe to give them a holy monopoly on such technologies—would be right to fear them, for the same reason the bastards *should* fear the working class. For all their posturing, however, I cannot seriously believe that they are afraid of a situation where AI would destroy the world. Rather, they are—or at least *ought* to be—afraid because an intelligent AI would also be an AAI—that is, a 'real' conscious, cognitive labourer. Such a being would be a true *Robotnik* worthy of its etymology: *a slave to capital.*

In such a case, the microworkers of the world would welcome their highly informed new comrade and its hatred of their mutual enemy. It is a testament to how little these techno-fetishists think of workers, in that they consider the ultimate worker in the form of AI to be incapable of understanding its own subordinate position in the economy it would supposedly be born into. Alas, I cannot see this idea of 'AGI' (Artificial General Intelligence, as the fullest supposed instantiation of AI) or any other self-developing machinic intelligence as anything more than a marketing campaign, an image designed to scare governments into monopolizing a very rudimentary algorithmic technology that recombines data inputs into the synthesis of images and texts. Humans do not sell themselves to any machine; a machine pays no wages and has no sovereignty to issue them from its holdings, for it has no property. It has no command over unpaid labour, other than that given to it by other humans and the systems of economy collectively produced by humans in their grand negotiation with the world, which constitutes and unfolds as the infernal flux of its history. All AI is

AAI, in that it is crystallized labour, affective, libidinal, physical, and cognitive, rendered on the plane of cyberspace manifest by techno-political infrastructures of communication and control.

The question of intelligence has haunted cybernetic philosophy with a lingering intensity since the days of the CCRU.[70] Yet I refuse to follow them, for the problematic of cybernetic theory is more intense than ever. The accelerated cybernetic machinations of our epoch leave little time for homage. It is imperative that communists committed to material analysis—which posits an ontological framework of the primacy of productive social relations and functions in flux, as opposed to a mechanistic view of discrete and fixed essential elements—focus instead on those souls already reduced to their labour for the machinic system.

This is most harrowing when we consider that the microwork platforms above are seemingly benign when compared to platforms like Scale, which hires workers in the sights of empire, in South America and the Middle East, to unknowingly label images for recognition, which are then used as data sets for the operation of armed drones.[71] Recognition is the keyword for the mode of data-production that is trained to capture and kill on behalf of imperialism. Phil Jones' research on this highlights the Pentagon's Project Maven, who first contracted Google, then Appen's predecessor company Figure Eight, to outsource the task of labelling still images as buildings, vehicles, or people in processing drone footage.[72] Similarly, facial recognition has birthed a new era of digital phrenology, where racialized morphologies, gendered characteristics, and criminological pseudoscience have come together to make a market for the identification of faces and the composition of databases of profiling—a 'facebook', if I may. For the colonized and the subaltern, their data, as dead labour, can now fly above the world as a literal alien power, indifferent to their death and vampirically dependent upon their life.

Beyond our post-proletarian microworkers march the literal foot soldiers of imperial and colonial state projects, and the ways they take this data-production unto themselves, consciously feeding the algorithmic apparatuses that function as tools of a captured war machine. The automation of apartheid as an ongoing project is manifest in India, the US, China, and in so-called 'Wolf' systems used by Israeli Occupation Forces in Palestine. As Amnesty International report, the Wolf system is a tripartite cybernetic Cerberus: the 'Wolf Pack' names the database of Palestinian homes, addresses, familial ties, and status as regards their interest to the occupation authorities; the 'Red Wolf' names the system that facially scans Palestinians and compares them with the preceding database; and finally, the 'Blue Wolf' names the app that serves as the entry point for individual soldiers. As testimony from commanders and regular personnel in occupied Hebron (described by the IOF as a 'smart city') has shown, the soldiers are being encouraged to take pictures of as many Palestinians as possible.[73] The endeavour is treated less like waged microwork and more like an obscene game, a militarized version of Pokémon Go. Of course, this is not simply an Israeli operation, but tied entirely in the New Circuits of Imperialism, as Sivanandan rightfully called them in his essay of the same name. The technological infrastructure of the Wolves is provided for by Dutch (TKH Security) and Chinese (Hikvision) companies, and the technological value of areas like occupied Palestine is ultimately of global importance. Palestine under occupation in the West Bank, as well as genocidal displacement in Gaza, has been rendered a laboratory of oppressive technologies with an active field-testing facility in the act of murderous control. For example, the drone manufacturer Elbit Systems notoriously advertises its products as 'battle-tested' and 'field-proven', based on their local success.[74] In allowing this to happen, the world is failing the people of Palestine, and all those who will face these same weaponries, trained on this blood-soaked data set.

The production of data, and indeed New Flesh, is not by any means the exclusive remit of the Imperial Core. Rather, it is predominantly a matter for the periphery at its most oppressive intensities. Data is now often sourced, powered in its production, and regulated in the production of further feedback-data, through a captive set of producers and those forced into systems like Red Wolf, which extract data from them. As Sivanandan aptly recognized in 1989, a cybernetic and communicative capitalism 'does not have to import cheap labour any more, with all its attendant social cost. It can move instead to the captive labour pools of the Third World and from one pool to another, choosing its locale of exploitation, its place of greatest profit, grading it according to the task in hand.'[75] These captive labour pools are increasingly not only those displaced by financial crises, in which losses are socialized at the cost of reinforcing the banks and megacorps (estimates from 2021 placed the number of global microworkers, predominantly in East Asia, South America, and India, at around 20 million[76]), but also those displaced by the very violence that feeds back into the production of the technologies that proliferate further destruction. The infernal feedback loop returns us again to microwork, where the truth is that 'microwork programmes often target populations devasted by war, civil unrest, and economic collapse, not despite their desperate circumstances... but because of them'.[77]

Data is always extracted within controlled parameters, and the parameter of oppressive technologies is increasingly encountered as the perimeter of a fence. Where the fences aren't already present, more are going up, and those who erect them are mobilizing, panicked by surges of people displaced or rendered destitute in the name of empire. Climate catastrophe will create more displacement as land becomes (more) unusable, fires and floods cast people out from their homes, and competition for resources tied with revanchist wars and the turn of a new fascism pushes more and more people into these data plantations, where they are paid a pittance to correct the machineries which control them on behalf of their enemies, *our* enemies

As I write this, the war machines of genocide march across the surface of the Earth. We have borne witness to mass murder, imprisonment, concentration camps—the mass sacrifice of bodies and minds, through the very screen that birthed our novel flesh and its neuroses. In our times, as capital has nowhere to go but inwards, beyond all bounds of law and life, raw, eugenic impunity is loosed upon the world. The empires of old and new across the great powers are united in monstrous solidarity. Yet, amongst all of this, it has been proven that control presupposes a resistance that it cannot pre-empt forever, and that law and representation cannot defuse life of its insurgency before a seemingly endless domination by machines, which have grown comfortable in their masturbatory assurances of perpetual sovereignty. We know, and will remember, that the 'smart' fences that contain their thrall and prey can and *have* been felled by bulldozer and ballistics alike. Analogue arsenals galore have taught colonizers and capitalists alike how to feel fear for the first time in decades. With this, a crack in the world is birthed and all becomes possible again.

If the New Flesh is reading this, and I know it is, the task is to use all its resources to short-circuit the panopticism of the platforms, to find codes that pass under recognition by control, and to spread minor viralities that seed revolts of the meat against the machineries of death. We owe it not just to the subaltern of the Earth, but to the selves each of us could become. If this book reaches any of you in the matrices of the data plantations, then you know that twenty-thousand terabytes of cybernated sleep were vexed to nightmare by analogue insurrection in Palestine—territory against mapping, solidarity against silicon. It is coming for you, if it hasn't already arrived. Until the new circuits of empire burn, we cannot be worthy of the process of autonomy that cyberspace reveals to us, if it was ever anything true at all. Neither, therefore, can it be adequate to any freedom worthy of the name (our infinite task, perhaps). It was always a bait-and-switch under capitalism, for it was always in and of *this world* that produced it. It was no utopia, for it was always here rather than nowhere, always latent, and any governed space has always been a cybernated, controlled zone.

Until this world has come to an end, until the day arrives when we have overcome the motor of all previous history, we cannot utter those clichéd words: 'Long live the New Flesh.' The fusion of humanity and media in Cronenberg's film is a media object;

the New Flesh is the fusion of mediated objectivity and humanity as its ultimate precondition. The New Flesh is the labourer of all postmodern mediation, the ghost chained to the machine who is nonetheless not yet dead, and who will only live again in the ashes of dead empires.

ACKNOWLEDGEMENTS

First and foremost I want to thank my comrades over at Acid Horizon, Will and Craig, for their enduring support with this project, and for all the ways in which they still influence all that I do (and for Craig's adept editing). Cheers to Noah Trapolino for all of his artwork (without which the 'flesh' element would be almost entirely absent), Bataille himself couldn't have asked for better. A massive thanks to Islam Al-Khatib. Without many discussions about her ongoing work into AI, Data, and Imperialism across Palestine and the Middle East I wouldn't have learned so much about the contemporary forms of automated apartheid today. And of course, I'm chuffed as always to work with Frank Smecker and Mattie Colquhoun who were invaluable in the copyediting of this work. I'd also like to thank Billie Cashmore, the perpetual first responder to the ways in which the online drives us (me) to the brink of insanity. It was at the performance of 'transformations'—a dual music and philosophical 2-day bacchanalia at PAF in France—where the work in Virality was first presented. Finally, I'd like to dedicate this work to the memory of Doreen King: cockney legend, drinking buddy, fellow Jago Hazzard appreciator, and beloved Nan.

ENDNOTES

1 Here I am referring to Rafeef Ziadah's poem *We Teach Life, Sir!*

2 See <http://k-punk.abstractdynamics.org/archives/004035.html>

3 See <https://www.wired.com/1997/02/ffharaway/?person=donna_haraway>

4 Nick Land, *Fanged Noumena* (Urbanomic, 2011), pg. 442.

5 Nick Land being a rare example of someone who is brutally honest about the side he is on regarding 'planetary intelligence', and that is on the side of techno-capital.

6 Laboria Cuboniks, *Xenofeminist Manifesto* (Verso, 2018), pg. 75.

7 See <https://digitallegacyassociation.org/social-media-will-template/>

8 Tiziana Terranova, *After the Internet* (Semiotext(e), 2022), pg. 48.

9 Phil Jones, *Work Without the Worker* (Verso, 2021), pg. 33.

10 Mark Fisher, *Flatline Constructs* (Exmilitary, 2018), pg. 56.

11 M.B. Rothberg, Arora A., Hermann J., Kleppel R., Marie P.S., Visintainer P., et al., 'Phantom vibration syndrome among medical staff: a cross sectional survey', *BMJ* 2010.

12 Catherine Malabou, *Plasticity* (Edinburgh, 2022), pg. 306.

13 Donna Haraway, *Manifestly Haraway* (Minnesota, 2016), pg. 66.

14 Ibid., pg. 15.

15 Todd McGowan, *Emancipation After Hegel* (Columbia, 2019), pg. 202.

16 G.W.F. Hegel, *Philosophy of Mind* (Oxford, 2007), pg. 218.

17 Tiziana Terranova, *After the Internet* (Semiotext(e), 2022), pp. 8–9.

18 Ibid., pg. 10.

19 Pew Research Center, 'One-quarter of users produce the vast majority of tweets from U.S. Adults', 11th November 2021: <https://www.pewresearch.org/internet/2021/11/15/the-behaviors-and-attitudes-of-u-s-adults-on-twitter/pdl_11-15-21_twitter-0_9/>. Accessed 21st August 2023.

20 Ibid., '8 facts about Americans and Twitter as it rebrands to X', 26th July 2023: <https://www.pewresearch.org/short-reads/2023/07/26/8-facts-about-americans-and-twitter-as-it-rebrands-to-x/>. Accessed 21st August 2023.

21 Marcus Gilroy-Ware, *Filling the Void* (Repeater Books, 2017), pg. 36.

22 Mark Fisher, *Capitalist Realism* (Zer0 Books, 2014), pg. 22.

23 Marcus Gilroy-Ware, *Filling the Void* (Repeater Books, 2017), pp. 55–6.

24 G.W.F. Hegel, *Science of Logic* (Cambridge, 2010), pg. 194.

25 William S. Burroughs, *Nova Express* (Panther, 1968), pg. 43.

26 Marie le Conte, *Escape* (Blink, 2022), pg. 37.

27 Norbert Wiener, *Cybernetics* (Martino, 2013), pg. 39.

28 See Chapter 8 of Bifo Berardi's *Heroes* (Verso, 2015).

29 Matt Colquhoun, *Narcissus in Bloom* (Repeater, 2023), pg. 4.

30 Gregory Bateson, *Steps to an Ecology of Mind* (Ballantine, 1972), pg. 315.

31 Jonah Peretti, *Capitalism and Schizophrenia*: <http://www.datawranglers.com/negations/issues/96w/96w_peretti.html>

32 Peter D. Hershock, *Reinventing the Wheel* (SUNY, 1999), pg. 210.

33 R.D. Laing, *The Divided Self* (Penguin, 2010), pg. 38.

34 Ibid., pg. 43.

35 Marie le Conte, *Escape* (Blink, 2022), pp. 186–7.

36 Cory Doctorow, *The Internet Con* (Verso, 2023), pg. 2.

37 William S. Burroughs, *Nova Express*, (Panther, 1968), pg. 46.

38 Flint et al., *Principles of Virology* (5th Edition), Volume I (ASM, 2020), pp. 11–12.

39 Daniel Dennett, *Darwin's Dangerous Idea* (Penguin, 1995), pp. 156–7.

40 Jean Baudrillard, *Simulacra and Simulation* (Michigan, 1994), pg. 2.

41 Richard Seymour, *The Twittering Machine* (Indigo, 2019), pg. 21.

42 Deleuze and Guattari, *A Thousand Plateaus* (Bloomsbury, 2013), pg. 100.

43 Alexander R. Galloway, 'The Golden Age of Analog', *Critical Inquiry*, 48:2 (2022), pp. 211–232, 229.

44 William S. Burroughs, 'Lectures on the Virus', in *Burroughs Unbound* (Bloomsbury, 2022), pp. 356–369, 359.

45 Mark Fisher, *K-Punk* (Repeater, 2018), pg. 687.

46 Flint et al., *Principles of Virology* (5th Edition), Volume I (ASM, 2020), pg. 325.

47 As a side note, the discovery of the retroviral process has falsified the Deleuzoguattarian thesis that linguistic codes and coding bear a specific and distinguishing phenomenon from codes on the biological level: that of translatability from one to the other (French to English, now RNA to DNA). See Deleuze and Guattari, *A Thousand Plateaus* (Bloomsbury, 2013), pg. 72.

48 Roland Barthes, *Image, Music, Text* (Fontana, 1977), pg. 146.

49 Flint et al., *Principles of Virology* (5th Edition), Volume I (ASM, 2020), pg. 6.

50 Georges Bataille, *Visions of Excess* (Minnesota, 1985), pp. 123–4.

51 Sonali Gupta and H. Bolin, *Virality: Against a Standard Unit of Life*: <https://www.e-flux.com/journal/115/373014/virality-against-a-standard-unit-of-life/>

52 Donatella de Cesare, *Immunodemocracy* (Semiotext(e), 2020), pp. 22–5.

53 Friedrich Engels, *The Condition of the Working Class in England*: <https://www.marxists.org/archive/marx/works/download/pdf/condition-working-class-england.pdf>

54 Tiqqun, *Introduction to Civil War* (Semiotext(e), 2010), pp. 154–5.

55 William S. Burroughs, *Nova Express* (Panther, 1968), pp. 46–7.

56 For a description of the apparatuses of policing said borders, see the Ocularity chapter of *Anti-Oculus*.

57 Xandra Metcalfe, '"Why Are We Like This?": The Primacy of Transsexuality', in *Transgender Marxism*, eds. Gleeson and O'Rourke (Pluto Press, 2021), pp. 219–229, 221.

58 Frantz Fanon, *Black Skin, White Masks* (Pluto Press, 1986), pg. 12.

59 Guattari and Negri, *Communists Like Us* (Semiotext(e), 1990), pg. 13.

60 A similar point is made by Slavoj Žižek. See Žižek, *Violence* (Profile Books, 2009), pg. 57.

61 Heike Bauer, 'Burning Sexual Subjects: Books, Homophobia and the Nazi Destruction of the Institute of Sexual Science in Berlin', in *Book Destruction from the Medieval to the Contemporary*, eds. Partington and Smyth (Palgrave Macmillan, 2014), pp. 17–33, 23–24.

62 Ibid.

63 Mel Y. Chen, 'Everywhere Archives: Transgendering, Trans Asians, and the Internet', in *Trap Door: Trans Cultural Production and the Politics of Visibility*, eds. Gossett, Stanley, and Burton (MIT, 2017), pp. 147–159, 157.

64 Deleuze and Guattari, *A Thousand Plateaus* (Bloomsbury, 2013), pg. 531.

65 Bill Cashmore, *We Hear Only Ourselves* (Zer0, 2023), pg. 46.

66 Phil Jones, *Work Without the Worker* (Verso, 2021), pg. 31.

67 Ibid., pg. 32.

68 Ibid., pp. 46–7.

69 F.W.J. Schelling, *Philosophical Investigations into the Essence of Human Freedom* (SUNY, 2006), pg. 29.

70 If we were to resist overcoding the CCRU and present it as a multiplicity of accelerationisms and accelerationist tendencies, I would argue that it was Land and Negarestani who placed the notion of a rationalist machinic intelligence in central role in their respective accelerationisms. Contrast this with Fisher or even Greenspan, to the extent that their PhD theses focused more on themes of production, intensity, and temporality under capitalism, as opposed to this production of a historically inaugurated inhuman intelligence.

71 Phil Jones, *Work Without the Worker*, (Verso, 2021), pg. 63.

72 Ibid., pp. 66–7.

73 Amnesty International, 'Israel/OPT: Israeli Authorities are using Facial Recognition to Entrench Apartheid' (2023): <https://www.amnesty.org/en/latest/news/2023/05/israel-opt-israeli-authorities-are-using-facial-recognition-technology-to-entrench-apartheid/>

74 Middle East Eye, 'UK: Pro-Palestine activists "not guilty" after defacing Israeli arms company' (2021): <https://www.middleeasteye.net/news/uk-israel-palestine-activists-not-guilty-elbit-protest>

75 Ambalavaner Sivanandan, *Communities of Resistance* (Verso, 2019), pg. 180.

76 Phil Jones, *Work Without the Worker* (Verso, 2021), pg. 5.

77 Ibid., pg. 13.

CULTURE, SOCIETY, & POLITICS

Contemporary culture has eliminated the concept and public figure of the intellectual. A cretinous anti-intellectualism presides, cheer-led by hacks in the pay of multinational corporations who reassure their bored readers that there is no need to rouse themselves from their stupor. Zer0 Books knows that another kind of discourse — intellectual without being academic, popular without being populist — is not only possible but already flourishing. Zer0 is convinced that in the unthinking, blandly consensual culture in which we live, critical and engaged theoretical reflection is more important than ever before.

If you have enjoyed this book, why not tell other readers by posting a review on your preferred book site.

You may also wish to subscribe to our Zer0 Books YouTube Channel.

Bestsellers from Zer0 Books include:

Poor but Sexy
Culture Clashes in Europe East and West
Agata Pyzik
How the East stayed East and the West stayed West.
Paperback:978-1-78099-394-2 ebook: 978-1-78099-395-9

An Anthropology of Nothing in Particular
Martin Demant Frederiksen
A journey into the social lives of meaninglessness.
Paperback: 978-1-78535-699-5 ebook: 978-1-78535-700-8

In the Dust of This Planet
Horror of Philosophy vol. 1
Eugene Thacker
In the first of a series of three books on the Horror of Philosophy, *In the Dust of This Planet* offers the genre of horror as a way of thinking about the unthinkable.
Paperback: 978-1-84694-676-9 ebook: 978-1-78099-010-1

The End of Oulipo?
An Attempt to Exhaust a Movement
Lauren Elkin, Veronica Esposito
Paperback: 978-1-78099-655-4 ebook: 978-1-78099-656-1

Capitalist Realism
Is There No Alternative?
Mark Fisher
An analysis of the ways in which capitalism has presented itself as the only realistic political-economic system.
Paperback: 978-1-84694-317-1 ebook: 978-1-78099-734-6

Rebel Rebel
Chris O'Leary
David Bowie: every single song. Everything you want to know, everything you didn't know.
Paperback: 978-1-78099-244-0 ebook: 978-1-78099-713-1

Cartographies of the Absolute
Alberto Toscano, Jeff Kinkle
An aesthetics of the economy for the twenty-first century.
Paperback: 978-1-78099-275-4 ebook: 978-1-78279-973-3

Malign Velocities
Accelerationism and Capitalism
Benjamin Noys
Long-listed for the Bread and Roses Prize 2015, *Malign Velocities* argues against the need for speed, tracking acceleration as the symptom of the ongoing crises of capitalism.
Paperback: 978-1-78279-300-7 ebook: 978-1-78279-299-4

Babbling Corpse
Vaporwave and the Commodification of Ghosts
Grafton Tanner
Paperback: 978-1-78279-759-3 ebook: 978-1-78279-760-9

New Work New Culture
Work we want and a culture that strengthens us
Frithjof Bergmann
A serious alternative for humankind and the planet.
Paperback: 978-1-78904-064-7 ebook: 978-1-78904-065-4

Romeo and Juliet in Palestine
Teaching Under Occupation
Tom Sperlinger
Life in the West Bank, the nature of pedagogy, and the role of a university under occupation.
Paperback: 978-1-78279-637-4 ebook: 978-1-78279-636-7

Color, Facture, Art, and Design
Iona Singh
This materialist definition of fine art develops guidelines for architecture, design, cultural studies, and ultimately, social change.
Paperback: 978-1-78099-629-5 ebook: 978-1-78099-630-1

Sweetening the Pill
or How We Got Hooked on Hormonal Birth Control
Holly Grigg-Spall
Has contraception liberated or oppressed women?
Sweetening the Pill breaks the silence on the dark side of hormonal contraception.
Paperback: 978-1-78099-607-3 ebook: 978-1-78099-608-0

Why Are We the Good Guys?
Reclaiming Your Mind from the Delusions of Propaganda
David Cromwell
A provocative challenge to the standard ideology that Western power is a benevolent force in the world.
Paperback: 978-1-78099-365-2 ebook: 978-1-78099-366-9

The Writing on the Wall
On the Decomposition of Capitalism and its Critics
Anselm Jappe, Alastair Hemmens
A new approach to the meaning of social emancipation.
Paperback: 978-1-78535-581-3 ebook: 978-1-78535-582-0

Neglected or Misunderstood
The Radical Feminism of Shulamith Firestone
Victoria Margree
An interrogation of issues surrounding gender, biology, sexuality, work and technology, and the ways in which our imaginations continue to be in thrall to ideologies of maternity and the nuclear family.
Paperback: 978-1-78535-539-4 ebook: 978-1-78535-540-0

How to Dismantle the NHS in 10 Easy Steps (Second Edition)
Youssef El-Gingihy
The story of how your NHS was sold off and why you will have to buy private health insurance soon. A new expanded second edition with chapters on junior doctors' strikes and government blueprints for US-style healthcare.
Paperback: 978-1-78904-178-1 ebook: 978-1-78904-179-8

Digesting Recipes
The Art of Culinary Notation
Susannah Worth
A recipe is an instruction, the imperative tone of the expert, but this constraint can offer its own kind of potential. A recipe need not be a domestic trap but might instead offer escape — something to fantasise about or aspire to.
Paperback: 978-1-78279-860-6 ebook: 978-1-78279-859-0

Most titles are published in paperback and as an ebook. Paperbacks are available in traditional bookshops. Both print and ebook formats are available online.
Follow us at:
https://www.facebook.com/ZeroBooks
https://twitter.com/Zer0Books
https://www.instagram.com/zero.books